DOING CHRISTIAN EDUCATION IN NEW WAYS

DOING CHRISTIAN EDUCATION IN NEW WAYS

EVELYN M. HUBER

Judson Press ® Valley Forge

DOING CHRISTIAN EDUCATION IN NEW WAYS

Copyright © 1978
Judson Press, Valley Forge, PA 19481

All rights reserved. No part of this publication may be reproduced, stored in a retrieval system, or transmitted in any form or by any means, electronic, mechanical, photocopying, recording, or otherwise, without the prior permission of the copyright owner, except for brief quotations included in a review of the book.

Library of Congress Cataloging in Publication Data

Huber, Evelyn.
  Doing Christian education in new ways.

    Bibliography: p. 111.
    1. Christian education. 2. Christian education—Teaching methods. I. Title.
BV1471.2.H79   268   77-13390
ISBN 0-8170-0782-2

The name JUDSON PRESS is registered as a trademark in the U.S. Patent Office.
Printed in the U.S.A.

This book is dedicated to staff members, both past and present, of the Division of Church Education, Board of Educational Ministries, who have given me encouragement in my search for effective ways to nurture all persons in the Christian faith. Also, it is dedicated to all church educators who continually try to find the best approach to education in the church.

Contents

1	Introduction	9
2	Guidelines for Selecting and Developing Educational Models	13
3	Description of Models	17
4	How to Start a New Model and Maintain It	27
5	Models for Staffing Educational Programs	33
6	Illustrations of Alternate Models	37
	List of Alternate Models	110
	Bibliography	111

1

Introduction

There are many questions and some excitement in churches today about alternative models or forms for the church's educational ministry. The term "alternative" or "new" usually is used in contrast to the traditional church school. Terms like "open education," "discovery learning," and "learning centers" are heard often when church educators, lay and professional, get together. Piaget, Erikson, and Dewey are referred to by many church educators as well as by public educators. Many articles have been written about using these persons' learning and developmental theories in the church.

Most of the suggestions for educational innovations in the church today are based on the concept of "open education." A philosophy of "open education" calls for classroom or teaching space which is not bound by chairs in rows or by very small rooms assigned to an individual teacher and class. "Open education" means that the learning opportunities are based on the fact that persons learn from their own doing, not someone else's. It means there is variety in the way persons can study a particular subject. This Chinese proverb is descriptive of the philosophy upon which the open education approach is planned.

> I hear, and I forget;
> I see, and I remember;
> I do, and I understand.

Some churches have tried new forms with success. Others have tried the same forms and have experienced dissatisfaction and sometimes despair. There is an element of risk in trying anything new. However, the teaching ministry of the church is too important to continue doing things as usual if they are now ineffective, no matter how effective they were in the past. Selecting a new model is not a put-down of the model for teaching that the church has been using. For merely moving to a new form is not always the answer either. It certainly will not be the answer if the change is made without adequate research on needs of the learners and if adequate interpretation and preparation are not made. Inadequate preparation does not take seriously the importance of the church's present teaching ministry or its future ministry. Inadequate planning does an injustice to the new form and the old form. Both the appeal and the threat, the strengths and limitations of the new, need to be examined early in the planning process.

This book is an attempt to assist churches in more carefully planning how they will do Christian education. The term "model" means: *SHAPE OR DESIGN.* For example, the traditional church school is a model. The church school is shaped by a weekly meeting, usually on Sunday; classes for all ages, like in a public school; and usually classes which meet for one hour. Although some churches have found ways to alter this basic design of the church school to meet their particular needs, for the most part, this model is typical across the country. There is a feeling of being "at home" in the Sunday church school. However, the kind of learning that takes place in that familiar model will vary from church to church and sometimes from class to class within the same church.

By suggesting alternative models, we are not saying that the traditional is not a good model. For many churches, it still meets their needs. For other churches, it is meeting the educational needs of a portion of the congregation. For still others, even reshaping the traditional model is not sufficient to revitalize the teaching ministry or to meet persons' educational needs. Some churches have changed to a new model for their teaching. Other churches will, with purpose, have two models for their teaching program because of the great diversity of educational needs and interests in their congregations. A congregation needs to be intentional about whatever model it chooses. With intentionality, it can hold on to the old and use it wisely or change to something new without loss of learning for those who are involved.

"Models" or "forms" are used henceforth in this book to refer to the church doing Christian education by different groupings of persons, at different times of the day or week, in less structured meetings, or in more open ways of learning. Such changes are appealing to many.

What This Book Is
—It is an "idea starter," a stimulator.
—It is a resource to assist a church in planning the next year's Christian education program.
—It offers guidelines for selecting a new model of education.
—It is reports of churches who have been innovative in Christian education.
—It is material to be examined, studied, and adapted.
—It is material which can be used when a church wishes to reorganize completely its Christian education program or renew its existing program.
—It is a guideline for preparing a congregation for change.
—It is a way of thinking about education and of selecting alternative models for education.

This book does not promise success to any church which tries a new model. It is only a resource.

The Kind of Church the Book Is For
—It is for the church whose existing educational program is going well; however, some of its members are not being reached by its existing programs.
—It is for the church in which some of the educational programs are going well, and some are not.
—It is for a church which is seeking a change in its educational approach for summer.
—It is for the church which wants to look at new types of learning groups, new ways of grouping people for learning, or new ways of learning.
—It is for the church where there is dissatisfaction and unrest with the Christian education program.
—It is for the church which has a strong Christian education program and wants to keep it that way.

Some Ways to Use This Book
—Read through it for ideas.
—Quickly answer for yourself the questions raised in the section

"Guidelines for Selecting and Developing Educational Models."
—Have the book reviewed at the annual Christian education planning meeting.
—Reflect on how the suggestions might enrich Christian education in your church.
—Examine what other churches are doing to meet educational needs, and let your mind "walk around" some of these ideas to see how they look.

2

Guidelines for Selecting and Developing Educational Models

Any model (shape or design) used for education in the church, whether a new model or one of the familiar models, should be selected and developed on the basis of the church's overall goal for Christian education and objectives for a particular year. One model or several models may be used to assist the church in meeting its educational objectives.

The decision for selecting and developing any educational model or models is based on the response the educational leaders give to these four questions.
- What is education?
- What are learning and knowledge?
- What is the role of the teacher/leader in the learning process?
- What is the role of the group in the learning process?

Here are two illustrations of what certain responses to the above questions would mean.

Illustration One[1]

What is education?   Does the church view education as transmission of knowledge and information about the Bible, church history, and the heritage of Christianity? Does it view knowing Bible content (stories and facts) as the most essential part of education?

[1] This matrix is adapted from one designed by Patricia Minuchin, Temple University, Philadelphia, Pennsylvania.

What are learning and knowledge?

Does a church think religious learning and knowledge are knowing biblical content? For example, are biblical learning and knowledge a person's ability to repeat the Ten Commandments, his or her ability to quote verses he or she has memorized from the New Testament and selected Psalms, or his or her ability to name the books of the Bible? Are learning and knowledge thought to have taken place when students are able to tell a certain number of biblical stories or identify biblical characters? Is the concept of knowledge confined to identifying some of Jesus' teachings or naming some of his miracles?

What is the role of the teacher/leader in the learning process?

Is the teacher seen as the "director" of learning? Does the church believe the teacher's role is to present the material which is to be learned, to listen to the repetition of the memorized passages or the rehearsal of facts? Does it see the teacher's role as judge of when the student has learned?

What is the role of the group in the learning process?

Does the church see the role of the learning group, the class, as very secondary, possibly even irrelevant, to the process of learning? If this is so, individuals might as well study alone with a teacher as attend a class. Is the class considered just a convenient way to group persons who are learning?

If a church answers these or similar questions affirmatively, then that church will do well to choose a model which allows for the opportunity for learning facts efficiently, a model which places a high value on these facts and information. A church holding the above views must understand that its educational ministry would require rewards and the withholding of rewards for learning, a kind of behavioral modification teaching-learning. The teacher becomes important as a giver of facts but not necessarily as a person to whom to relate on an interpersonal level. If experiencing Christian community is not seen as important, then a teacher-controlled class or group is acceptable.

A church may with good cause desire to transmit knowledge and information. This in itself is not bad. However, emphasis on this kind of a fact-oriented, teacher-controlled model would rule out the opportunity to relate biblical truths to life and limit opportunities for students to test the validity of the truths for their own value system.

Programmed instruction, which is one form of this learning process, can be usefully incorporated into more open designs or models and used when facts are needed and useful. Programmed instruction provides a quick way to learn needed facts. The role of the teacher who has facts and a faith to share with students is important in the church's teaching ministry.

Illustration Two

What is education?	Does the church believe education is helping persons to be sensitive; to relate Christian teaching to life; to recognize themselves as unique persons, children of God? Does the church view each person as a unique individual with special skills, abilities, gifts given by God? Does the church believe the purpose of education is to enable persons to be involved in mission and to use their gifts?
What are learning and knowledge?	Does the church view learning and knowledge as discoveries of the relationship between facts and ideas? Does it believe biblical knowledge can be used for problem solving in everyday situations and for value development? Does it view Christian learning as making choices, questioning, inquiring, searching, and resolving? Does the church see learning as a consolidation of facts through many media into useful, meaningful insights of life? Does the church believe that learning takes place when the learner is involved in a life situation,

then reflects on the involvement in relation to biblical truth, and gains personal meaning from the experience and the reflection?

What is the role of the teacher/leader in the learning process?

Is the teacher seen as being a model human being, as providing material and a process for learning that is relevant? Is the teacher one who helps to develop a climate that is conducive to learning? Is the teacher seen as one who has a faith to share? Is the teacher viewed as a learner along with other learners? Is the teacher viewed as one who supports the individual learner and the group? Is the leader seen as one who mediates between members of the group who are in conflict and who helps the members learn from their conflict?

What is the role of the group in the learning process?

Does the church see the group, or class, as central to the learning process? Does it believe that the group, or class, is a small society in which Christian relationships are discovered and experienced? Is the group seen as open to experimenting with and testing values? Does the church believe that persons can learn from their peers as well as the teacher, or leader?

If a church can answer affirmatively the above or similar questions, it will select a model that allows for flexibility and openness. It will select a model which provides for involvement of and interaction between members of the class, between the teacher and the members, and between resources and media and the members. Openness does not mean that there is no structure or that there is no content with which to deal. Open models allow the class to be very intentional about what is to be taught and learned, and then how it is to be taught and learned.

3

Description of Models

Using the definition of a model given earlier in this book, "shape or design," this resource deals with examples of models with a more open approach. It discusses a variety of ways to organize the teaching-learning group; it describes alternate models of how learning takes place; it discusses flexibility in ways of grouping persons for learning; and it suggests alternate times for conducting the learning groups.

The Shape or Design for the Teaching-Learning Group
Contract Teaching

An agreement is made between the individual learner and the teacher. Contracts are written which state what the learners agree to study and how that study will be done. It is a plan in which the learners set the goals and direction for their learning. The teacher contracts to provide the resources for study and to share in the learning process. For an illustration of *contract teaching,* see in chapter 6 of this book the section entitled "Church Schools Don't Need to Die." The administration is open, allowing the learners choices and space in which to do their own learning. This more open model allows opportunity for the class, or group, to experience the church as a faith community.

Individualized Instruction

Individualized instruction can operate within a group structure or can be a completely solo experience. Individualized instruction in the church presupposes content and concepts about the Christian faith that each person should learn. A program of study for the individual is based on the person's present knowledge and what else the person wishes to know. The individual sets learning goals and selects the ways those goals will be achieved. The leader provides the needed resources, plans for evaluation and feedback, and provides a community setting where learnings can be shared and practiced. Individualized instruction is similar in many ways to the process used in Contract Teaching. Also, it can be incorporated as a part of a learning center model.

Learning Centers

> A learning center is an area in a classroom containing a collection of activities and materials to teach, reinforce, and enrich a skill or concept. It may be located on the wall, on a table, in a corner, on a rug, in a hallway, or elsewhere. Activities and materials placed in a center are designed to teach a specific skill or concept, and thus they are based on specific learning outcomes. A learning center usually includes several stations that cover a topic or aspect of a topic, a concept, or a group of skills.[2]

A learning center is a place or designated area where the learner can work toward a specific learning goal. A particular center may be used by one or more persons at a given time. Individuals may use several centers during a particular study. This is perhaps the most familiar of all the models described here. See the article in chapter 6 entitled "So You Want to Try Learning Centers." Other resources for learning centers are given in the bibliography.

School of Religion

In a School of Religion model, a year or more of courses of study are selected. The courses of study are planned not only to cover a wide range of interests but also to provide for progression in the content and the depth at which the content is studied. The series of courses is the curriculum for the School of Religion. Descriptions for the courses are written. From these curriculum descriptions, persons attending the school select their courses of study. Based on the school concept, prerequisites for some courses may be necessary. However, for the most part, those attending can choose what they will study on

---

[2] Richard C. Ishler, Margaret F. Ishler, and Phyllis Lamb, *First Steps to Open Classrooms in the Church* (Chicago: The Arizona Experiment [National Teacher Education Project], 1974), p. 9.

the basis of when a certain course will be given and their own needs. Courses of study for Schools of Religion vary. Some churches may offer only biblical studies, while others may plan a School of Religion on human and social issues, such as peace, liberation, justice, racism, world food crisis, and human sexuality. Other churches may build a curriculum which combines biblical studies and human and social issues.

Festival/Celebration

In this model, the study course is organized to follow the church year, special religious festivals, and/or significant events in the life of the local congregation. Reformation, Advent, Easter, and Pentecost are liturgical seasons to be celebrated or observed as festivals. The significance of the event is studied (including its theological and historical base). A celebration of the event is planned in a manner which is in keeping with the particular group's experience. Persons create music, drama, art, poetry, or prose to express their understanding of the relationship of the gospel and Christian teaching with the event. Sharing the creative expressions with the entire congregation or segments of the congregation can also be a part of the celebration or festival.

This model is an example of what is to be studied shaping the manner in which the study is conducted. One church intentionally built into its church school curriculum a celebration every seventh week. A celebrative mood was created by the various groups sharing their learnings of the previous six weeks through songs, stories, skits, art work, etc.

Models for How Learning Takes Place
Action-Reflection Method of Learning

Action-Reflection is a process persons use to learn. Drawing from the words "action-reflection" to define the process, we get the picture that the learner is involved in the activity or an experience or a project. The learner then uses an organized process to think about what happened or did not happen in the experience. The learner looks at what happened in the light of his or her learning goals and the goals of the project or activity. Were they achieved, and, if not, what hindered the successful achievement of the goals? An example of this method is a group entering into a project to bring about political change in a community or to develop a self-help program for a community of people. When the project is finished, or even while the group is still engaged in it, time is given to reflection on the theological meaning of being involved and to identification of the relationship between the project and the Christian gospel. Often the reflection is done through biblical study and input from reading and sharing.

The Inquiry or Discovery Method of Learning

This method of learning starts with a question to be answered or a problem to be solved. Something is recognized as being "not right," and the study group works to find a solution. Christian values and biblical teachings are used to help find the solution. The same process can be followed when students identify questions about faith and its teachings. The question or questions are researched to find satisfactory answers.

The Shape or Design of Meeting Time

When a church examines its educational needs, it may find that its time schedule is adequate. Or it may find that the time or times of meeting(s) are not convenient for all of its people. There are a number of possibilities open to a church which is not locked into one time or day for its teaching ministry.

Weekdays

Elementary grade children's and youth's study sessions can be held after school or early in the evenings. Adult groups can meet at night or at an early breakfast once a week. Sessions for preschool children can be conducted for half of a day during the week. However, weekday schools are usually not as feasible for a church in which the congregation travels great distances to attend activities. They are more difficult to use if a number of school districts are involved. In a church where this model was successful with children and youth, the attendance of individuals was more consistent than on Sunday. One value of a weekday school is that the pastor can more easily be involved as a group leader.

Weekends

Study retreats four or five times a year can become the major time for teaching-learning for junior and senior highs or young adults. In some churches in which this has been tried, they use the traditional hour on Sunday for youth choir rehearsal or for service projects. It has been found that retreats, which combine recreation and study, can provide more time for in-depth study than meeting once a week with spasmodic attendance. For an example of this model, read the article "Retreats—An Answer to Your Group Slump?" in chapter 6.

Saturdays

This one day can be used in a variety of ways beyond just changing the meeting day from Sunday morning to Saturday morning. There is more flexibility in a Saturday school than in a Sunday school. For instance, one Saturday a month for three hours, every Saturday for one hour, or every other Saturday for two hours are schedules which can be used on Saturday but might not be possible on Sunday. See the articles "A Saturday Church School" and "Big Tuesday" in chapter 6.

Summer

Special study programs or study tours during the summer can become alternates to a year-round program. Such programs can also be supplements to the year-round program. The familiar models are the vacation church school and day camp. Mission study or service tours and work-study projects are possibilities for summer. Some local churches have developed their own camping program in addition to the state or regional camps.

School Vacation Times

There are areas in the country where every eight or ten weeks the public schools have a week of vacation. This time could be used by a church. A one-half day or a full day during each of the school vacation periods could become open for teaching-learning.

Models for Alternate Groupings of People

Most churches will not deem it wise to do away completely with peer educational groups because peer relationships are very important. In peer learning groups, these relationships often develop. Groupings of peers, however, can take place within the context of either an intergenerational or a broadly graded group. Two types of models are described here.

Groups for a Variety of Ages
Intergenerational

An intergenerational group may include a clustering of people of a variety of ages. The clusters may be youth and adults; children and youth; children and adults; or children, youth, and adults. Intergenerational groups may include only complete families, families and single persons, or portions of families. In each intergenerational group, each child and/or young person should have one or two others who are approximately the same age. This intergenerational model is sometimes called the "extended family." This model, where successfully used, has illustrated that persons of differing ages can learn with one another and from one another.

Ungraded or Broadly Graded Groupings

Here are examples of persons of various ages grouped in some way other than a class for each age group. All preschool children including kindergarten can be put in one group and children, grades 1 through 6, in another. Kindergarten children through sixth grade in one group is possible. Kindergarten through grade 2, and grades 3 through 6 is another way of grouping. Youth, in grades 7 through 12, can be placed in one group for learning. A church could follow the model of four groups: nursery and kindergarten, grades 1-5, grades 6-8, and 9-12. In each of these patterns, subgroups of persons who are near the same age or skill can be provided. This kind of regrouping of age calls for the use of one of the more open and flexible designs or models.

Family Clustering

The Family Cluster Program consists of four or five units (single person, widow, widower, divorced person, any group of persons living together, nuclear family) meeting together over an extended period of time for shared learning experiences. Ten weeks is often considered a basic time limit.

A trained leader with a co-leader assumes prime responsibility for the cluster as it becomes a community. Leadership, then, often becomes shared by group members.

Some objectives of a cluster are:
1. To provide an intergenerational group of families who share their values and insights.
2. To provide a group setting which can grow in support and mutuality.
3. To provide an opportunity for families to consider together serious topics.
4. To provide an opportunity for families to model aspects of their family systems for each other.

5. To provide perspective for parents to observe their children in relationship to other children, and likewise, children to observe their parents.

Most clusters meet for a supper between 6:00 and 8:00 P.M. with each family bringing its own meal. Times of singing, games, and family sharing are included, and the evening ends with families often celebrating their being together.

Most educational experiences are chosen so that the youngest to the oldest may participate at his or her own level of experience and maturity. For more information, contact Dr. Margaret Sawin, Family Clustering, Inc., P.O. Box 18074, Rochester, NY 14618.

Groups for Special Interests or Needs

Groups for Parents

A model which is not always examined by a church is one of planning learning groups around parents. Such groupings might be: single parents, parents with preschool children, parents whose oldest child is a teenager, parents with only teenage children, and parents who have just had their first child. Such groups are reformed as the status of the members changes. Curriculum is selected to relate to special concerns and interests of the members of the group.

Special Interest Groups

Some examples of special interest groups in a church are listed here. Boards of the church can become study groups as well as work and service groups. People in the same vocation and persons who united with the church at the same time (a continuation of membership/discipleship classes) can be grouped together. Groups can be organized for persons who are handicapped. Some people always have to work on Sunday but can meet during the week or on Sunday evenings for study. The teachers and leaders of the educational programs of the church may meet regularly for study and support.

A word about meeting place. Any of the models or forms suggested above will require a board or committee of Christian education to examine the use of the facilities available and possibly make some reassignment of space. At no time should an assumption be made that a model is not possible because of limitations of the church's building. Wait until a study is made. However, it can be disastrous to make complete plans for a change only to find space is not available or, if available, that arrangements have not been made for its use. It was mentioned earlier that some models described in this book can be incorporated into an already existing educational model. A way to look at the models suggested is to see how they might be used in the existing church school or in a new educational group. New programs can be started for persons not presently attending the traditional church school, or who cannot attend at the appointed hour, or who seem to be losing interest. A new model is often a way to attract persons who seem disenchanted with a church's teaching ministry.

The following listing may help the reader see opportunity for use of the various models:

Renewal of the Church School
1. Learning centers in some or all classes; regrouping regular classes to use learning centers.
2. Contract teaching-learning with a few classes or with a group of individuals in one class or in different classes.
3. Individualized instruction within classes or with selected individuals from any class.
4. School of Religion or a series of elective courses for youth, adults, or youth and adults together.
5. Festivals/celebrations as part of the regular study of existing classes.
6. Weekday instead of Sunday school for all or part of the church school, e.g., the elementary grades and/or youth grades.
7. Weekend retreats for study using the Sunday church school time for other activities.
8. Ungraded or broadly graded study groups where the number of available students is small.
9. Saturday school for all or part of the classes.
10. A different teaching model for the summer months or for six weeks in the middle of winter.
11. A month, perhaps between two semesters or two quarters, for a church's mission study program.

New Educational Programs
1. Individualized instruction for persons who have dropped out of church school or who are losing interest.
2. New groups (short term or long term) for persons in the same vocations, single parents, persons who have recently had deaths in the family, new members in the church, etc. These groups could be formed for community and could use individualized instruction or contract teaching so the teaching-learning could cover individual needs.
3. A School of Religion.
4. Use of the school vacation times throughout the year for major teaching-learning opportunities for youth instead of traditional church school on Sunday.
5. Extended family groups.
6. Intergenerational groups.
7. Family clusters.
8. Use of special church celebrations or the church liturgical year to interest persons who have dropped out of traditional church school.
9. A mission tour or a work-study tour to replace a regular study program or to involve church school dropouts.

Chapter 6 of this book gives illustrations of how churches have used some of the models described here.

Curriculum and the Nontraditional Models

The selection of curriculum resources is very important, and the decision concerning curriculum resources is made on the basis of how the resources can help a church achieve its goal for Christian education. Never should curriculum resources dictate the shape or design of a church's educational program. Most curriculum resources are more flexible than we have sometimes thought. When a church is considering the possibility of a new model either to strengthen its existing church school or to start a new educational program, it may very well discover that its present resources are most usable. In fact, there are very few complete curriculum resources prepared and labeled as such for learning centers, intergenerational groups, schools of religion, parents' groups, etc. Since the development of most curriculum resources is based on key religious themes, how persons learn, and how these themes relate to the persistent life issues of individuals, these resources can be used with most models. Some adaptations are necessary, but many teachers find this necessary when using any prepared curriculum.

Most of the alternate models suggested usually can involve persons from a broader age span in the same learning groups. Therefore, leaders of these models have a broader base from which to select resources and teaching ideas. Curriculum materials prepared for all the ages involved can be used.

In the bibliography there is a limited list of curriculum resources which are specifically prepared for some models.

4

How to Start a New Model and Maintain It

Preparation is the key word for starting a new model. Preparation of leaders; of the participants; of the congregation; and, where children and teenagers are involved, of the parents is most important.

One of the first steps in the early planning stage is the naming of a coordinator or supervisor if the model is being used for a new program. This is the key to the implementation of the planning. If the model is to be used in the church school setting, the church school superintendent would be the coordinator or supervisor. The coordinator of a model which calls for a new time or setting will report to the board or committee of Christian education just as the church school superintendent or coordinator does. The new model coordinator and the leaders with whom he or she works can also expect support from the board or committee of Christian education similar to that which is given to the church school leader.

Often it is desirable to try a new model for a specific time period. This would be especially true if it is hoped that the model or a variation of it might become the major teaching-learning program of the church. For instance, a church might try the intergenerational or extended family model during the summer months, for the Christmas season, or during Lent and Easter. Another possibility is that during special seasons of the church year the children's classes could be broadly graded and learning centers used.

An example of one church's preparation to move to learning centers for a portion of its elementary grades provides a specific illustration of adequate preparation. When the First Baptist Church of Worcester, Massachusetts, made such a move, they followed this plan.

First, the teachers who were to be involved were introduced to the learning center model by using it to learn about learning centers.

Second, the preparation of the congregation, including the parents, was done through a brochure which described what learning centers are and gave general information about how the model would operate in that church. Explanation was given of the role of the learner and the role of the teacher. The church's goal for Christian education and a description of the three units of study for the next five or six months were included.

The brochure also included the plan to be used for introducing learning centers to the children. That part of the brochure is included here in its entirety because it is very thorough and clear.

PLAN FOR TRAINING CHILDREN TO USE THE LEARNING CENTERS

Needs: To "own" the concept.
  To learn how to achieve learning objectives.
  To learn acceptable use of the freedom implicit in the "open" concept.

Goal: To introduce open education to the children in a manner that enables them to see its worth and make it work.

Objectives:
  Show children the purpose and value of open education.
  Enlist the enthusiasm of the children.
  Provide them with skills needed to meet their commitments.
  Build a sense of responsibility in using time, supplies, and resources.

Strategies:
  Each class (grades 3-6) will "walk" through the Learning Center concept with the following purposes in mind:
    To teach them experientially about learning centers through storytelling, filmstrips, etc.
    To express learning via drawing, painting, etc.
    To show use of resources and media—what is expected.
    To allow children to evaluate the experience.

Schedule for the introduction:

December 1	Grades 5 and 6
December 8	Grade 4
December 15	Grade 3
January 5	Grades 4 and 6
January 12	Grades 3 and 5

Complete interpretation of a model can lessen the threat a new model may bring to other parts of the church's educational program. Also, it will lessen any anxiety persons have about moving into something new.

When You Are Ready to Launch a New Model

When, in your regular planning process for Christian education, it is evident that some change in the way of doing Christian education will enrich your educational program, the following steps should be taken:

1. Have the members of the board or committee on Christian education, educational teachers or leaders, and the pastor respond to the questions in the chapter entitled "Guidelines for Selecting and Developing Educational Models."

2. Select the model(s) which seems to meet your needs from the illustrations, or develop your adaptation from these models.

3. Study the resources which are available describing that model. Some information on models as well as illustrations are given in chapter 6 of this book. You may also refer to the bibliography which is included at the end of this book.

4. Finalize plans for use of the model, including the selection, recruitment, and training of leaders.

5. Plan how you will prepare the congregation for the change. Outline how you will interpret the model and its program to the participants and, in the case of children and youth, how you will interpret it to their parents.

6. Determine when evaluation of the model and its teaching-learning role will be made. Periodic evaluation is helpful when something new is started. Evaluation of the new model will be conducted when the total Christian education program is evaluated each year.

Maintaining a New Model

The task of establishing a new model of education and keeping that model healthy requires at least four levels of maintenance. This kind of care is really relevant to any form of educational ministry, but the need is highlighted and must be especially planned for when there is a move away from the traditional or familiar forms of education. These maintenance levels are: assign administrative responsibility; secure and use periodic feedback and evaluation; plan support for the leadership; and build identity for the model.

Administrative Responsibility

The new model of education in a church will of course be developed and launched by the board or committee on Christian education, since this group is responsible for all policy and administrative decisions. It is the responsibility of that group to select the coordinator/supervisor/superintendent of the new model. This is the person or persons who will care for the day-by-day, week-by-week details. It is fair to assume that any new model will require the same kind of administrative personnel as the Sunday church school and the vacation church school, two familiar models. In fact, a new model may need more administrative attention in the early stages of its life.

Feedback and Evaluation

There needs to be built into the planning of all educational models opportunity for evaluation. The most effective education includes feedback from the participants and the leaders on the learning that is taking place and on how well the program is operating. This is even more essential when a church is using an educational model or method which it has not tried before. It is not only necessary to receive but also to act upon the feedback given so that the model can respond to persons' needs.

Support of Leadership

Too often innovative persons are thought to be self-sufficient. Therefore, a person accepting a leadership role in a new model may be seen as not needing support or training. But all leaders need a support system for effective functioning. A church moving to a new model for part or all of its educational program needs to make sure that the leaders receive training in the skills needed to implement the model. The leaders need to know that there are persons who will listen to their ideas and their concerns. They need to know that there are persons who share in the responsibility for the desired outcome of the model. Leaders need to know that there is a backup for times of crisis or expansion.

Identity Building

One of the strengths of the church school as a model is its long history. Persons, some even with unhappy memories of church school, will testify that the church school has had an important place in their lives. It has an influential place in the history of the church. People who have attended it can identify with the name "church school" and with what happens there.

A new model which calls for a new group of people and possibly a new time of meeting needs to claim a membership for itself and develop a self-conscious image of itself as a learning group. This will take time, but it must happen. Adequate interpretation of the new model and its educational objectives at the time of inauguration will help the model establish an identity.

If a new model and a traditional model are both part of a church's educational program, they need to be seen as equal. Reporting to the congregation concerning the growth and development of the new group will identify the new model and its membership as an integral part of the church's educational ministry.

5

Models for Staffing Educational Programs

The familiar style of one teacher or even two teachers for one age group or class is only one way to staff a church's educational program. In some cases, this model is possible, and it works. On the other hand, for a variety of reasons, churches have been led to experiment with plans for staffing the church school and other programs for education. Some of these new models have been used successfully.

Each church needs to develop its own philosophy about its style for staffing its educational program. Even if the plan of one teacher for one group for a whole year is working for a church, that church may wish to explore additional or alternate ways to involve persons in leadership roles in its educational ministry.

The team concept of leadership for groups is probably one of the most popular models. Team teaching, several teachers teaching together in one group or class, is not a new concept. It may take a variety of forms as we will see later. These persons see themselves as "the teachers." They study and plan together. They share the various classroom responsibilities. They share responsibility for personal contacts with the learners, and they evaluate together. This is the picture of the way any successful team works.

Teams can be formed in several different ways, even though any team will need to work together as just described. The ideal, of course, is a team made up of the same persons working with one class or group for a full year. The ideal is often not possible; so churches look for other options (such as the following) for forming teams.

Option I. A complete team for a year with sufficient members allows each team member to have some time away from the teaching-learning group. A schedule is set up to insure that a complete team is present each time the group meets.

Option II. Team Leader or Co-Leaders serve for a full year. This person (or persons) is a permanent member(s) of the team. As many additional team members as are needed for the size and type of the learning group are enlisted. All or some of these may serve part-time. The length of service for members of the team may be determined by the individual's special skills and interests. A particular issue in the course of study may call for a team member with special information or knowledge. Another factor which may determine when a team member will serve may be the amount of time that person can give to the teaching-learning group.

Option III. Two complete teams are formed for one group for the year. One team is responsible for the teaching-learning group the first half of the year and the other team takes over for the second half. An alternative possibility in this option is that the teams rotate their responsibilities by units of study or periods of time. Another alternative is one team of leaders for nine months and a second team for the three summer months.

The options described for teams can also become models for staffing one-leader groups. Even very dedicated persons sometimes feel the need for refreshment and growth. One teacher can be responsible for one period of time and another for the next period.

Churches using the school of religion model or elective subjects for classes have already built in a rotational plan for leaders, since the leaders would be selected on the basis of their special abilities and knowledge in a particular field.

There are values to team leadership. Some may seem obvious; others will surface as a church uses team leadership. Some of the values are:
- shared responsibility
- more opportunity for breathing space or time off from the group which meets each week
- more ideas and additional ways of looking at an issue, which results in a wider variety of learning activities for the group.
- a better ratio of teacher to students, thus, providing far more individual attention

- a sense of community is very important where volunteers are concerned—in a team, there is opportunity to build community
- opportunity for children and youth to experience more than one example of a Christian adult

The more open models for education call for more teachers and resource persons, so a team is advisable. Also, models such as learning centers and individualized instruction are very demanding on a leader's time. A team to share these demands makes serving as a teacher more viable for the average, volunteer lay leader.

6

Illustrations of Alternate Models

While a model or models for the educational program of one church cannot be used in the exact form by another church, a description of such models can stimulate a church's thinking about ways to do Christian education.

In this chapter there are descriptions of ways that different churches have used to carry out their educational programs. Some of these became the form for the church's major Christian education program. Other churches used a new model to renew their church school or to revitalize their youth ministry. Others used a new form to augment parts or all of their educational program.

There has been a considerable time lag between the research of various models and the production of this book. Therefore, some of the illustrations in this section may not be in operation now. This does not make the model invalid, nor does it indicate that the church was necessarily disenchanted with its experience. Changes may have been made to respond to new educational needs of the congregation.

The stories from churches are presented according to the following categories (see p. 110 for a complete list of alternate models):

        Learning Centers
        Other Alternative Models
        Models for New Groupings of People
        Alternative Meeting Times
        Celebrations/Festivals
        Model for Staffing Programs

Learning Centers

SO YOU WANT TO TRY LEARNING CENTERS[3]
by Iris L. Ferren

The room was humming with activity and conversation. There seemed to be almost constant movement. A lot of different things were going on at once. To the visitor used to quiet and order, it was pandemonium. To the children and teachers in the learning center for grades one through three, it was fun, exciting, and interesting.

The unit was on following Jesus' way at play and around home. The children moved from one center to another as they chose, exploring the theme in many ways. The teachers moved about the room, answering questions, asking questions to stimulate thinking, suggesting a possible next activity to the child who couldn't decide, and helping children identify what they were learning. For the four-week unit the room was set up with a number of centers, including a game designed to point up decisions for the use of time. In another center, a filmstrip portrayed different situations with the endings to be worked out by the viewer. There was a cassette tape recording of a story from the children's study book to listen to with some questions to think about, Bibles and guidance for doing Bible study, supplies and directions for making puppets or dolls to illustrate the Bible stories, a table for writing and drawing. A conversation area provided space for everyone to gather for the last ten to fifteen minutes. On one wall was a long sheet of paper on which had been printed the unit theme and several goals and questions to explore. This is the way one church developed a learning center approach.

Learning centers are not new. They have been recommended and widely used for many years with preschool children. In more recent years, many have seen the advantages for elementary children, youth, and even adults. The central idea is to provide simultaneous activities or ways to explore a theme; the learner chooses from among the different options.

The learning center approach is not an easy way out of the problem of lack of interest in church school and declining attendance. Its demands are high on both learners and teachers. Learners are called upon to take responsibility, to make decisions, and to become involved in learning. They can't just come and sit or goof off. They have to participate in determining directions both for the total group and for their own exploration. Teachers are required to spend

[3] Reprinted from *Baptist Leader*, July, 1975, pp. 2-5.

considerable time in planning and preparing for a unit. For example, one two-hour workshop using learning centers required about seventy hours of planning and preparation, but there was little to be done during the workshop itself. In fact, the leadership team of three almost felt left out of the fun people were having as they followed the directions provided in each center. Once under way, the major responsibility of teachers is to remain sensitive and alert to the progress individual learners make and the problems into which they run. On occasion, they may serve as special resource people. It is not so much what the teacher's guide or plan calls for, but what learners are saying by their comments, expressions, and actions that is the concern of the teacher. This approach is particularly enhanced by and really dependent upon respect for the worth, individuality, and creativeness of each person, whether that person be a teacher or a learner. It may take some time for learners and teachers to grow into this approach. But despite the discipline, the decisions, and the hard work, many find the rewards of increased interest and enthusiasm worth the effort.

Very little curriculum material is provided for the learning center approach although many materials provide resources which can be adapted or at least used as a starting place. Thus, some creative work on the part of the teachers/planners is necessary. How do you go about it?

First, determine the focus of the unit and some learning goals or aims that are appropriate for the age of the learners and the amount of time available for the unit and which are in line with what is known about the members of the learning group. Most curriculum materials will assist in this step. However, any aims, goals, or purposes given in curriculum materials need to be rewritten in terms of the particular group and situation. Goals or aims may be stated as questions, as projects to be carried out, or as a point to reach. Other aims may be added as plans are made for specific centers. It would be a good idea to put the theme or focus and the goals on a large sheet of paper and place this so it is in full view of the group throughout the unit. These spell out the destination. Members will take different ways of getting to the destination, and they may not all land on exactly the same spot, but they'll need to know whether they're going to New York, San Francisco, Miami, or Dodge City. Teachers and a class should not hesitate to spend a whole session on this step, especially where everyone makes a contract with oneself and the group regarding what one wants to work on. This provides much of the motivation, the reason for becoming involved in the unit and selecting a learning center.

A second step is that of deciding the general way to set up the learning centers. At least eight different ways can be identified, and there could be combinations of these eight. The choices at this point will make considerable differences in the planning and preparation that follow.

1. Centers may be set up so that learners make a decision at the first session on a center or activity and stay with it throughout the rest of the sessions designated for the unit. This assumes that it is not essential for each learner to work on the content or the particular activity of every center. Sometimes a closing session is designed to provide opportunity for those in each center to share some of their experience and learnings with the total group, thus making it possible for everyone to have some exposure to the content, projects, or activities of the total unit.
2. Centers may be set up with the expectation that learners will work in several centers during the course of the unit, moving from one to the other according to interest. A particular learner does not have to work in every center in this case and may even elect to spend all of his or her time in just one. Centers under this plan usually require less time for completion than those identified above. The group described at the beginning of this article was working in this fashion.
3. Centers may be set up so that it is necessary for each learner to work in each center during the course of the unit, but he or she may do so in the order he or she chooses. For example, one center could provide resources and guidance for studying the background and facts related to a particular biblical passage, the Book of Jonah, for instance. Another center could focus on present-day situations which are related to the biblical passage. Resources for this could include films, magazine and newspaper articles, and recorded interviews regarding present-day social issues, together with some questions and exercises to get at feelings and attitudes. Another center might include resources for working on projects. In the case of Jonah, this might include such projects as a paraphrase of the book, a film or slide set portraying the meaning of the story in present-day situations, letters to congressmen stating the writer's position on a particular issue, research into community problems and ways they could be met. While there might be a preferred order for working in these three centers, it would be possible to

begin with any one of the three and move to the others.
4. Centers may be built around aspects of a theme. The theme may be Christian responsibility in relation to current social issues. Each center could focus on a different social issue. A variety of methods and ways could be used in each. Each would need to provide a way to explore the factors in the issue, to examine one's feelings and attitudes related to it, to identify various ways to meet or resolve the issue, and to clarify one's own position regarding it. If at all possible, each center should provide a means of doing something about the issue as well as studying it. A concluding session could provide opportunity for sharing with the total group, but this is not always necessary. Sometimes the informal sharing members of a group do at other times will be sufficient. Displays about the room and throughout the church building are also ways of sharing.
5. Centers may be built around methods, with each center focusing on similar content. For example, the area of study might be the events in the last week of Jesus' life and their message for today. One center could use drama, another art, another film, another creative writing, and another music. In this case, learners select a center on the basis of the method they would like to use. The choice would be made, and persons would stay in the same center for the duration of the unit.
6. Each learning center may have a teacher assigned to it. The teacher carries responsibility of planning and preparing for the group's work in the center. Members of the group should be encouraged to contribute to the plans and preparation as much as possible, however. Sometimes the teacher is there because of a skill in a particular area, such as creative drama. It is possible to recruit persons for this type of leadership on a short-term basis, especially for those skills the more permanent team does not have.
7. Guidance for each center could be written out or put on a cassette tape. This assumes that the learners are old enough to read, to follow directions, and to work on their own. Roving teachers assist this process. In the learning center described at the beginning, the teachers had prepared instructions for each center. Some were taped. This made it possible for them to provide many more centers than there were teachers. A ninety-minute media workshop was set up and led by one person with taped or written instructions for some twenty different centers.
8. Some centers, especially those set up for young children, will need

very little guidance or instruction. However, a teacher in such centers as housekeeping, blocks, "dress up," or nature is needed to capture and take advantage of the learning moments. This need could be met by roving teachers.

Once the decision has been made regarding the way in which the centers will be set up, the designing moves to the task of determining the learning methods and the resources needed for each center. The resources should include guidance as well as the materials with which to work. For instance, in designing the twenty-odd centers for the media workshop, the instructions were given on a cassette tape for some and on typewritten sheets for others. The center on making color lift-off slides included illustrated instructions in chart form and materials for making the slides as well as a biblical passage to read, with instructions to make a set of slides to illustrate it. As much as possible, the learning activities should be planned so that the learners are learning by doing, thinking, trying out, reflecting, evaluating, and clarifying. Some activities may be suitable for individual work and others for group work.

The introductory session should provide opportunity to identify with one or more of the goals or aims, to become acquainted with the overall plan for the unit and its centers, and to make individual decisions on beginning points. Children may want to have a look at each of the centers before making a decision. A concluding session should provide some opportunity to identify individual and group learnings. This may be done through conversation, a worksheet or evaluation form, and the sharing of work done.

By now it is obvious that teachers do not wait until Saturday night to start preparing for a learning center unit which is to begin the next morning! It takes time to prepare and gather the resources. And so, what may look to the casual observer like utter chaos is really planned, disciplined disorder. Back of it are several hours of planning, creating, and gathering of resources. Back of it is the commitment on the part of teachers and learners to goals and the investment of oneself in the achievement of them. And learning in the church takes on (perhaps) a new sense of excitement and fun.

"WE DECIDED TO TRY LEARNING CENTERS"[4]
by V. Rex Woods

It was obvious that something had to be done! The resistance to learning could be felt and seen almost as soon as one walked into our

[4] Reprinted from *Baptist Leader,* August, 1976, pp. 2-5.

church school classes, and the older the students got, the worse it became. Don't misunderstand me: There was no violence, no rowdyism—just a lot of *passive* resistance to the teacher, the material, the church in general, and, of course, to God's love for them and to his claims upon their lives. They just *sat* there. It was almost as if they came daring anybody and everybody to try to teach them anything—and it seemed that the students were winning. Need it be said that teacher recruitment was difficult, and that everybody's morale was low?

We had talked about some changes, but most of them seemed either superficial or overwhelming, and none of them held our attention for very long. Then nine people from our church—the entire board of Christian education, several teachers, and the pastor—attended a two-day workshop on learning centers, sponsored by our state Commission on Christian Education. The purpose of the workshop was to help participants learn about learning centers in and through the use thereof. According to our own interest or need, we read and listened to recordings; we looked at displays or watched a movie or some filmstrips; we discussed issues and questions and made puppets; and we learned how to make slides and how to prepare instructional objectives. We came away with a lot of questions—and with a lot of excitement about the possibilities that learning centers offered.

We had thought about learning centers before. They were being used in our public schoolrooms, and our six-year-old building had been designed with open and unstructured classroom space to facilitate their use. A former member of our board of Christian education had pioneered their use in our public schools. But we had been easily discouraged: We didn't have the leadership, or the right resource materials, or the budget, or enough students, or the courage to break new ground.

But now, we had seen and experienced the possibilities; furthermore, the issue was forced when two of our most creative teachers (whom we had sent to Green Lake Laboratory Schools in years past) said that they weren't sure that they would teach if we didn't use learning centers. So our board of Christian education approved using learning centers for the thirty youngsters in our church school in the first through sixth grades; it was also decided that we should use the curriculum which we were already using, for the most part. Three teachers were recruited who would work together as a team.

That summer the teachers began reviewing the student's and teacher's books of the curriculum for primaries, middlers, and juniors, noting course/unit titles and themes, goals, and any other ideas which intrigued or excited them, or which they thought would capture the attention of the students.

In August, the three teachers and the pastor sat down together to begin hammering out specific plans for the year. We began by identifying the overall course theme "Knowing the Living God" and discussing the ways in which the living God has made himself known to us through: the Scriptures, the natural world, our own experiences and relationships, history, and, especially, Jesus Christ. These seemed to delineate natural learning units; since we felt that the Bible could and would be used in each of these areas, we did not consider it as a separate unit.

We then took a look at our calendar for the year (our church school year begins on the Sunday after Labor Day and runs till the Sunday before the Memorial Day weekend), noting special days and seasons—Rally Day, Advent, Christmas, Lent, Easter, and our closing date. We decided to use the Advent and Lenten seasons as the periods when we would focus on knowing the living God through Jesus Christ; the other units then seemed to fall into place quite naturally. We would begin the year with two units on God's creation, concentrating first on the natural world and then on us as his children. Then would come Advent, followed by a long unit on God's self-revelation through some of the leading characters in biblical history; Lent and Easter would follow; and finally, our plans would call for the year to end with a unit on people who know God in a living way today.

Following this scheduling of units, we tried to define an overall objective for the year's course. It was clear that we wanted the students to have more than just "head knowledge" about God. We wanted them to *experience* him as well; and so, though we never found words to express it, the experiential aspect was included in our thoughts, because we felt that it helped define not only the content but also the style of our teaching relationships. We felt that, in terms of the natural order, awe is not so much taught and learned as it is shared; the same is true of faith, or love, or hope, or joy.

We struggled a lot with objectives, and though we sensed their importance, we felt even more the urgency to get on with our specific plans for the learning centers. The objectives, at best, always seemed a little vague. It was becoming obvious that time was passing by us, and that we still had a lot of work to do before the fall season began.

In the meantime, each of us had been generating a lot of ideas for activities which could help students develop an understanding of and perhaps even experience the living God in and through the natural world. We wrote down all these ideas; where there were similarities, we grouped them together until we had about a dozen groups. From these we selected the nine groups that best supported our objectives and were most within the limits of our capabilities to carry out.

We settled on nine groups (or learning centers) for two reasons: first, we only had space for about that many centers in our 30' x 40' room, and second, we had heard at the learning center workshop about a church that had used nine learning centers in a tick-tack-toe chart to help their students get started and to help give some structure to the learning experience. In order to complete a unit, a student had to complete three squares in a row—just like in the game. If they chose to, however, they could do more, as time and ability permitted. We used the following arrangement for our first unit:

Mural making or collages	Reading	Community action
Movies	Nature center	Acclimatization
Bible study	Field trips	Music and records

Of course, not all these activities could be available every week; and so each student, with the help of an adult, would have to work out his or her plans for the unit so that everything that was desired could be done. Most of the centers had a choice of several activities which students might do, depending on their individual interests and abilities.

After recruiting people to help set up and supervise each of the nine learning centers, we were ready—more or less—for the opening of the church school year. Each of the thirty children was assigned to one of the three lead teachers who would keep records of his or her goals, achievements, and progress and help each when necessary.

We had hardly begun our first unit (i.e., knowing God through nature) when we began planning for our second unit on knowing the living God through our experiences and relationships as his children. For this unit, the following tick-tack-toe was developed:

Games	Reading	Who am I?
Our senses	People	Picture stories
Bible study	Movies	Making and playing musical instruments

Again, there was a choice of activities in each center, according to the student's interest and abilities. For instance, nine members of our church came to the "People" center to tell about their work or hobby; a child had to talk to at least three persons to complete that square. In the "Who am I?" center, a person could make his or her own fingerprints, a shadow picture, or a body picture; identify baby photos; or have his or her picture taken and, with assistance, printed. We found that both plans worked well for a five-or six-week unit.

A new crew of leaders was recruited for the Advent unit in order to give our first-unit leaders a breather and enable them to begin planning for the next unit. In terms of identifying objectives, possible activities, etc., the pastor went through a similar planning process with these new leaders. This group chose to drop the tick-tack-toe plan, not only because we had such a short time span with which to work, but also because we chose as an objective the production of a pageant, something which had not been done in our church for a number of years.

After doing some Bible study together, the students were given several options—a puppet show, a choral reading, a shadow play, a slide show, or a play. They chose the last. Some of the youngsters wrote the play, while others prepared costumes and scenery—with adult help, of course. Those not involved in the production of the play formed a junior choir to sing with the production. The students were allowed to choose the parts that they would play in the pageant; the only hitch came when we had two girls who wanted to play Mary, but that was easily resolved. The pageant was presented in place of the sermon during the Sunday morning worship hour; there was minimal resistance, and there were no snags—a real tribute to what can happen when students, with adult support and help, are allowed to do what they want to do. Many of the students rated this activity as one of the things that they most enjoyed in the first four months of our new approach to church school.

A complete evaluation for us will come later, but some tentative observations are possible now.

On the positive side, our purchasing priorities have changed: we are buying less printed curriculum materials and more supplemental activity materials—filmstrips, craft and art materials, movie rentals, new books for the library, and so on. This has enriched our variety of activities considerably and has not taken anything away from the students. Another real plus came from one of our leaders who said that her Saturday evenings and Sunday mornings are far less hectic because her work is all done and more of the classroom responsibility is falling on the students. She reports that her husband and children have also appreciated this! One new family joined our church in large measure because they liked our church school program. And one "old-timer" (a junior member of our church school) said after her first Sunday using the learning centers, "I learned more today than I did all last year!"

On the other side, perhaps six years is too much of an age span to try to cover in one group; some of the younger children seem to be overwhelmed and lost, while some of the older ones feel that it's childish and beneath their dignity to be included with the younger ones. There are signs that some of this feeling is fading, however, and perhaps it is simply a first reaction to something that is new. Some parents and other adults feel that the students aren't learning anything but are simply enjoying themselves (and after our last few years, as described in my opening paragraph, I say, "Thank God for that, at least!"). We can't help but wonder how long it will be until our creativity dries up. We recognize that more advanced and outside preparation is required in learning centers, and we wonder whether we will have people willing to invest the necessary time and energy. And one of our major concerns is the matter of evaluating learning progress. More clearly defined learning objectives will help us evaluate what we have or have not done. It should be said that this situation of meaningful evaluation is not new, either with us or with a lot of other churches I have known.

When we began, we didn't know if we could succeed in such a program. None of us had worked with learning centers before, and we were all essentially amateurs in education. But those of us who have worked as leaders have found a lot of satisfaction in our own accomplishments as well as in the resurgent enthusiasm of the students. We've been fortunate because we've had a lot of things going for us. We've had two *good* leaders who have had Green Lake Lab School experience, and who have been willing to give time and energy and talent into making this work. They love children; they're willing to learn; they're willing to risk themselves in doing something new; and they're willing to work—hard! We also have an excellent classroom which is open and flexible, and we have excellent audiovisual supplies for a church our size. We also have a good working relationship with other churches so that we can borrow equipment, etc., from them. And we have a cooperative public library.

Learning centers involve a lot of work! Whether or not we will continue to use them, we don't know, but one thing is certain: We can't go back to where we were—and that's good!

CHURCH SCHOOL DOESN'T WANT TO DIE![5]
by Roger Price

Slipping attendance and bored students sliding out of class via daydreams and excuses don't need to be the marks of your senior high church school. And it won't be—if students' needs and their differences are taken into consideration. It must be remembered that all kids are not alike; that they don't always think alike and don't always like the same thing nor are they all at the same spot in their religious development. What's good for one youth may be entirely wrong for another. With this in mind, Mr. Price describes the new model of education that was initiated in his former church.

What Is It—This New Model?

It's called "discovery/learning." What does it mean? Students are given several study options from which to choose. They choose the study area that interests them most and proceed to explore that theme or concern in a variety of ways. One or several students may be involved in a study area. The emphasis is on the student, with competent adult guidance, to discover for himself or herself the meanings and conclusions of his or her study.

How Does It Work?

It took a series of teachers' meetings to get things started. First, we had to deal with the questions and anxieties of the teachers about this new approach compared with the traditional, graded system. Second, we had to establish the guidelines. It was our feeling that both teachers and students had to be involved in establishing curriculum and themes. However, the final responsibility was to rest with the adults.

[5] Reprinted from *Baptist Leader,* July, 1974, pp. 49-52.

For each of the study/learning centers there was to be a theme based on our church school curriculum. Using the curriculum in this way would also provide the teachers with some basic biblical resource helps. There were to be three to four learning centers offered each unit. The learning centers would be offered for a specific period of time—approximately eight weeks. Youth were free to choose one of the centers but had to stay with that choice for the allotted study time. At the end of the eight-week period, they would be free to choose from a new group of learning centers.

Since we were starting this approach in midyear, we would use the teachers already on our staff. They were a diverse group with a great deal of ability. Other teachers would be brought in on a short-term basis to help with a particular theme or learning center.

What Were the Learning Centers?

Eight centers are listed here, plus a description of what actually happened to the youth in them. Remember that only four were offered at a time.

Bible

This was a traditional study group. It was not the most popular at times, but it did serve a real need. It was there for those who wanted it and needed it. It was the right thing for some of our more conservative youth or those who had no church background and wanted to find out something about the Bible.

Thanksgiving

During the Thanksgiving season there was a center dealing with the meaning of "thanks." Some of the youth in this particular group decided to express their appreciation to a group of adults they liked. They did some work with biblical passages related to thankfulness and then made "appreciation cards." On the cover was a photo of the adult for whom it was made. On the inside was a biblical verse and a personal statement.

The group collected cameras, learned how to operate them, and began taking candid snapshots of their favorite adults. A lot of time was spent in sharing and discussing. When the project was completed, the youth personally delivered the "appreciation cards" to each adult. It was a great success and did much to build a sense of "community" between the youth and adults of the congregation.

Contemporary Literature

We took the theme of our curriculum and decided to see how it could be developed through general literature—fiction. We had a number of our youth interested in literature, and this proved to be a good way of dealing with their interest and the biblical theme.

Ecology

Another group—more activist minded—became interested in the ecology movement. They became concerned about the way things looked around the church—the outside of the building and in the community. They studied some of the factors involved in the disposal of trash. The city council at this time was considering a recommendation banning disposable bottles within the city. This was a project the youth in this group wanted to support, so they went to the city council meeting. However, they got the "brush-off" from city council. Instead of giving up, the group got angry and began sending representatives to every council meeting to raise the bottle issue. The council postponed debate on the issue time and time again. At one point, the vice president of the national glass company sent a representative to speak to them. Eventually, however, city council passed a compromise bill and afterward commended our youth for sticking with the issue. It was a great learning experience for the youth of that group, even though it took several months of hard work.

Christmas Action

During the Christmas season, one group lived out their faith by taking on several projects for some of the small children in the community.

Drama

Another group worked on drama and did some original creations using the theme that was in the church school materials.

Worship

One of the center themes was on worship, and this group really got into worship. They created and put together an original worship service for presentation to the church. They did an excellent job with it—proving that youth, when left to their creative instincts, can do some great things.

Ten Commandments

Another group (I was kind of worried about this one, too) was started as a study of the Ten Commandments. The group was composed of our "goof-offs," and we were afraid of what might happen in it. But our architect teacher, who was also a photographer, really came through. He challenged the group to put into visual image the Ten Commandments, and to do it in such a way that they would be easily understood. In other words, the members were to take pictures of modern-day life that illustrated each of the Ten Commandments. The youth discovered they didn't know the Ten Commandments as well as they thought. In fact, they didn't know them at all. In their search for photos, they ended up in all sorts of unusual places—the hospital, the police station, the golf course on Sunday morning. They created some good photos and later made a presentation to the church on how the Ten Commandments relate to life.

This was our basic structure. It worked well for us—in this moment of our history. Tomorrow may mean something else for us. However, we tried and will continue to try to be responsible in recognizing that not everybody learns the same way or at the same time.

The Kind of Teachers We Had

They were a diversified group. One was an architect; another was a housewife who had formerly taught business courses in high school. Another was an elementary school teacher who really liked senior highs, and the fourth was a computer programmer. All were under thirty-five (which really doesn't mean anything), and all had worked with the kids in a variety of experiences. They felt very comfortable with the youth, and the youth felt very comfortable with them. At times, we brought in additional teachers who could help us with one of the learning centers.

Why Did We Start?

We began this approach about four years ago. At that time we weren't really familiar with the "learning center" approach, but we had areas we needed to work on, and so we explored this kind of approach.

One reason we tried learning centers was that we had over twenty-five kids in the senior high on Sunday morning, which (at least for us) was a large group; and it was diverse. This is what pushed us into a learning center kind of approach. There was the usual intellectual diversity, probably no greater or no less than an average group might have. There was a great maturity diversity, immature tenth grade boys on one hand and some seniors who were talking about college on the other. About half the youth were from nonchurch backgrounds. They were youth who had begun coming on their own initiative. Their families usually had no involvement with any particular church. So, although some of our youth knew a lot about church and had always attended and some knew at least a few things about the Bible, others were completely ignorant. The traditional or average church school class in which everyone was asked to do the same thing at the same time did not seem to be the best approach. Another factor was simply that youth have different learning styles. Some learn best in a visual form; some respond to reading material; others like to discuss. We wanted to take seriously these youth and their differences.

There was also some pressure from the tenth graders. We had worked hard at building a real evening fellowship group of tenth, eleventh, and twelfth graders. They felt discriminated against when forced into a tenth grade class on Sunday morning. We had created maybe the biggest part of our problem. For some time we had worked with our youth on assuming responsibility for their own faith. The teachers were not there to give them a ready-made set of answers. The teachers were there to help them think through and honestly respond to their questions, thoughts, doubts, and affirmations.

By this time, our youth were really taking this approach seriously—they could say what they needed to say; they were free to struggle; and they could be honest with the teacher. This honesty also meant, then, that the youth were free to tell the teachers when they felt the teachers were wasting their time or were talking about trivia. If our youth were bored, they would let the teacher know about it. While this was often hard on the teacher's ego, it was still a great reality check for helping us as adults to stay with the youth. They pushed us when they didn't like what was happening. Taking all these factors into consideration, we finally decided to move from the traditional, graded class system to something else. The "interest groupings" of the "discovery/learning center" approach made the most sense to us, and so we tried it.

Other Alternative Models
CHURCH SCHOOLS DON'T NEED TO DIE[6]
by Anne Gilbert

Our junior highs are excited about church school! Yes, we are doing something different with our juniors and junior highs in Sunday church school! We are using contract teaching, a structured method of individualized learning in which the student pledges with himself or herself to carry out the directions of a given lesson unit. Would you like to see this method in action?

Let's look in on a class. Our class is held in a large basement room that also serves as the church dining room. We mix together juniors and junior highs. Church school begins at 9:30, but over half the students arrive early to begin on their work. Kathy and Sherry have just arrived. They are checking their names on the attendance chart and getting their shoe boxes from the supply closet. Each of the students has his or her own shoe box where he or she keeps all his or her supplies.

The Listening Center

Our room is divided into several activity centers. There is the Listening Center, where Peter, Doug, and Jeff are already listening to a tape of 2 Kings 5, the story of Naaman. Jeff got the tape from our tape file and has put it into the cassette player. Peter and Doug are adjusting their headphones and finding Second Kings in their Bibles so that they can follow along as they listen. We have two tape players that are connected to listening bars in this center. There are three sets of headphones for each listening bar so that up to six students can use this area at one time.

We produced our own tapes. Five people, both men and women, made them so that we would have variety in the voices. Besides the Bible readings, we also taped readings to accompany pictures and stories. The boys and girls like to listen with headphones, and most of them feel that the tape helps them to understand the Bible reading better as they follow the print.

The Quiet Place

Over here we have a 9' x 12' rug on the floor. We call this area the Quiet Place. It's the place for thinking, reading, quiet study. Some of the students like to work by themselves, while others prefer to work

---
[6] Reprinted from *Baptist Leader,* June, 1974, pp. 52-56.

with partners. We encourage students who are not good readers to work with someone who does read well.

It's not unusual to see some of the students sitting on the rug. The three girls over there—Betty, Kathy, and Eunice—started working on the rebus of Jonah last week. This rug is a good place for them to roll out the paper and work. Kathy is a fifth grader. Let's ask her what she likes about church school this year. **"I like the way we work on the contracts. I think it is easier, and I learn more,"** she answered.

We also use the Quiet Place for sharing and reflection at the end of the session. Once or twice a month the boys and girls will read stories or articles they have written or share some of their creative art work.

The Work Tables

In the middle of the room we have two round tables with chairs. The students can work anywhere they want to work. Tracy and Ellen usually work at this table.

"What are you girls doing?"

"We're working on a crossword puzzle. It's part of the contract on Elisha and the Family."

"What do you like best about church school this year, Ellen?"

"I like making things. You can work at your own speed and you can do whatever contract you like," she replied.

The light-haired boy working at the next table is Steve, an eighth grader. When church school was over last June, he told his mother that he wasn't coming any more. His mother didn't know what to do. If she forced him to come, he might turn against church. But she did want him in church with the rest of the family. Then one Sunday I asked her to help with this group for a month or two. Steve was listening as she told her husband about the group and what they would be doing. When she finished, Steve said, "I'll go!" Since then, he has been in church school just about every Sunday. At Christmastime, he was one of the coeditors of our Christmas newspaper, which featured various aspects of the wondrous birth of Jesus.

One of Steve's comments this year was, **"You know, when you read a Bible story in a book, listen to a tape of the Bible reading, and then see a filmstrip, you really know the story."**

The Reading Center

Over in this corner of the room is our Reading Center. In the bookcase we have Bible storybooks, Bible dictionaries, Bible atlases, and other reference books. The students are free to use them wherever they need to. We have not had any problem with students failing to return books to the library.

Kathy and Lenny are doing a word-study sheet at the library table. The students use these wall maps when they have a map study in their contract.

The Review Center

The long table against the wall is where the students go for their review. When they have finished all the activities on a contract, they take a test. The test covers the facts of the story as well as the purpose of the contract. The only time that students don't share information with one another is when they take a review. They can work together on every other part of the contract. Susan and Dick are doing reviews now. When they have finished, our pastor will correct them. This provides him with the opportunity to get to know these students better.

Activity Center

After they have finished the review and talked with the pastor, they do a craft project. This is our Activity Center, where we keep all our craft supplies. In the bookcase against the wall are all the materials needed to do any handwork project in the set of contracts we are using this quarter. Things usually go very smoothly in this area. On the wall we have samples of all the projects that go with the contracts.

Kevin and Tommy are painting plaques. We find that a long table with benches works well for handwork. Shawn and Richard are making foil pictures. If you notice, the boys outnumber the girls in our group. We have twenty-seven students, and seventeen are boys. We have very few absentees—perhaps two or three a week.

We had the pupils write an evaluation of the class in January. One of the questions was: What do you like best about church school this year? Richard's answer expressed the feelings of so many: **"You can work independently instead of dragging along in a book."**

With so many boys in our group, you might think we would have discipline problems. We don't. Last year, in traditional classrooms, we did have problems.

Filmstrip Center

I want to show you what we have in the kitchen. Since we can darken the room, we decided to set up the projector and screen there for the Filmstrip Center. Jody and Bruce are watching a filmstrip right now as they listen to the record that goes with it. All the boys like to run the projector. We taught them how to use all the machines the first week.

Mrs. Brown is working at the small table near the Activity Center with Jack, Jesse, and Nicky. These boys are retarded, but they, too, work on the contracts. They can't do everything, but they can look at filmstrips, listen to tapes, have the teacher read them stories, and make handwork projects. There are four teachers, and we take turns working with them each week. We care for these boys very much, and we want them to succeed at what they do. They enjoy coming to church school.

How Did Our Church Get Involved in Contract Teaching?

Last year our junior and junior high teachers were concerned about their classes. Three problems bothered us: first, the poor attitude and lack of interest among our students; second, the lack of basic Bible knowledge of students who had been in church school most of their lives; and third, the alarming rate at which we were losing our young people after they reached junior high.

We felt that there must be a way to reach these boys and girls. We heard about a church that was doing something different with their juniors. Three of us visited the church and learned that they were using a form of the "contract method" of teaching. We saw the potential in the method and decided to try to write our own contracts.

Two teachers, Mrs. Irish and Mrs. Hall, from the Little Falls Baptist Church in nearby Gorham joined us as we began our work. After several sessions of meeting together and of writing at home, we had a visitor at one of our meetings, Miss Margaret Douglass, a teacher in the Portland public school system. She was using the contract method of individualized teaching with her students at school. She was completely sold on the method in public school and very excited about adapting it for church school. She has taught in church school for years and was eager to try some of the new methods of teaching.

In the weeks that followed, I spent many hours with Miss Douglass asking questions and learning about the contract method of teaching. We decided on a format for our contracts, and I began the long task of rewriting into this new form the contracts that our group had worked on.

What are the results in our church school? We have never had such enthusiastic students and teachers. Parents tell us that for the first time their youth like coming to church school. One of our seventh grade boys, James, was sick with a cold one Saturday. He stayed in bed all day so that he wouldn't miss church school on Sunday. Last year his mother had to force him to come to church school. Kathy, an eighth grader, dropped out of church school two years ago. When her sixth grade sister told her what we were doing, she started coming again regularly. Shawn, a sixth grade boy, came back after having dropped out in second grade.

We do not feel that we have solved every problem. No method is perfect, and no method will reach every person, but we believe that this is one way in which the church can effectively transmit Bible knowledge to junior and junior high students and help them relate it to their lives. It is a good way for us and our church. Something similar might be good for you, too—and then again perhaps another model might fit your situation better.

INSTITUTE FOR CREATIVE LIVING[7]

Youth participating in this program will be asked to make a firm commitment to participate in all basic sessions. For each quarter, the sessions include a weekend followed by six Sunday evenings. Those completing the course will be awarded a certificate of completion.

This program will confront youth with challenging tasks and experiences designed to help them explore their inner resources for meeting challenges. It will help youth develop skills in a variety of fields—camping, survival, climbing, obstacle courses, team building, problem solving, planning, etc.

Staff: Shirley Anderson, Steve Barbee, Wendy Frazer, Leslie Leavenworth, Earl Sires, and others to be announced.

This program is limited to thirty youth: fifteen junior highs and fifteen senior highs. From sixteen dollars to twenty-five dollars per family per quarter will be charged. This fee includes weekend costs.
Fall Quarter. The Person: explores who I am and what I am capable of.
September 26-28 Weekend at Allegheny Forest.
Oct. 5, 12, 19, 26, Nov. 2, 9. Group sessions at the church.
Winter Quarter. The Community: explores how I function in a group as a team member.
Jan. 23-25 Winter Weekend

[7] Reprinted from a brochure used by the First Baptist Church of Cleveland, Ohio.

Feb. 1, 8, 15, 22, 29, Mar. 7. Group sessions at the church.
Spring Quarter. Systems Affecting Our Lives: explores how I can identify and use my resources for constructive influence in my home, school, church, nation.
March 26-28 Weekend.
April 4, 11, 25, May 2, 9, 16. Group sessions at the church.

RETREATS • AN ANSWER TO YOUR YOUTH GROUP SLUMP?[8]
by Jeff Jones

The Sunday evening youth group is in trouble in many places. Attendance is down. The interest level among those who do come is slipping. Competition for youth is keen. And adults in "high church places" can only shake their heads and wonder why "it's not like it used to be." Much of the blame is too often heaped on the head of the youth advisor . . . or denominational youth resources.

If your group is one of those "slumping groups," this article might help. The first step for you to take is to ask the question, "Why?" Why is the group falling off in attendance and interest? Do any of the following relate to your situation?

[ ] Do many of the youth live quite a distance from the church? Transportation is a problem.

[ ] Do other organizations keep them away? Scouts, clubs, etc.

[ ] Is Sunday night a "fun" night rather than a church night? They go to the movies, visit friends; a great television program is on.

[ ] Are they so busy during the week that they need Sunday evening for studying?

[ ] Do their families tend to do a lot of "family things" on the weekend: travel, talk, etc.?

[ ] Do your youth see much of each other during the week—or are they "strangers" who meet at church?

[ ] Are there many potential youth in the congregation—or are you at a low cycle in youth numbers?

[ ] What other factors may be influencing the decline of your group?

The answers to these questions should give you a pretty good idea of the external commitment and attitudes that influence involvement in the youth group. If you see a pattern developing—one that indicates other involvements are acting like a magnet to pull the

[8] Reprinted from *Baptist Leader,* May, 1975, pp. 57, 60.

youth away—then it may be time to do some restructuring.

If radical restructuring is needed, here's a radical idea. Discontinue the weekly meetings and try a retreat program. Base your youth program on several periodic retreats held through the year. You would be meeting less often—but for longer periods of time.

Before you say "No!" . . . keep on reading.

Holding several retreats on a regular basis during the year has a lot of advantages.
- It's easier for a youth to find five or six free weekends a year than always to be available on Sunday evening.
- The simple fact of being away from the church building will build interest and attract many youth.
- The longer periods of contact with each other will enable the youth to build deeper, fuller relationships.
- It will be possible to relate the gospel's message of love to these relationships in a context in which its value is readily recognized.
- A full weekend together enables the group to balance seriousness and fun, study and recreation—helping to take the dull and boring label off of religious activity.
- It will be easier to relate the Christian faith to the full spectrum of the youths' lives, not just a small section of it that happens a few hours each week.

The retreat approach will mean some changes in thinking.

| Youth work becomes an intensive, short-term experience rather than a continuing program. | Retreats will have to be seen by parents and youth as a meaningful educational and spiritual experience. |

Retreats are not a time to escape from school and home to have fun—but a time for growth in Christian fellowship. This does mean fun, but it also means a commitment to study and responsibility.

The church's financial commitment to youth work will probably have to be reassessed. Five retreats a year will undoubtedly cost more than the youth themselves can handle.

If the need in your church is evident and this change in youth programming is a possibility, here are some ways you might handle a retreat-based approach to youth ministry.

A September Retreat

After school has begun and things are beginning to settle down, have a weekend to get away together. Emphasize personal sharing and group life. Quite likely the youth have not seen each other regularly during the summer. Growth has taken place, so they're new people and it's a new group. Take time to get to know each other again—how is everyone different; what new experiences need to be shared, etc.? Think about the year ahead. What expectations are there? What hopes and desires? Use these as the basis for planning future youth retreats.

Retreats in December, February, and April

Based on the experience of the first retreat, plan others that will meet the needs of the youth group. These can run the gamut from Bible study to "getting along with parents." Use one to plan and/or rehearse for a Youth Sunday worship service. On another, emphasize the essentials of genuine Christian community: trust, concern, acceptance, love. Or—make a movie, write a play, develop new forms of mission for the group. The sky is the limit! On a weekend retreat there's plenty of planning time.

A Retreat in May or June

Before the year-end rush begins at school, have a final retreat of the year. Use it to reflect on the group's experiences together. What has involvement in the youth program during the past year meant? Growth has taken place over the year, so they're new people and it's a new group. Use this retreat to reflect on and celebrate your newness.

So far we haven't dealt with the disadvantages of this type of approach to youth ministry. There are a number, but you can get around most of them.

How Do You Build Any Continuity Between Retreats?

It's a lot easier to develop continuity in group life than you might think—especially if you use the beginning of each retreat to get people on board with one another. One way is to present movies, slides, and photos of the last retreat. Have a time to share "photo memories" with each other. Additional ways will grow out of the group's experience together. It might be a song, a game, an activity, or a ritual (such as raising the group's own flag). All these things are a way of saying, "We're here now; it's time to begin." And more importantly, each of the youth thus relates this retreat to past experiences, so you are not faced with the impossible task of beginning all over again.

How Do You Cope with the Natural Desire of Youth to Stay Up All Night Whenever They're Away from Home?

The best solution to this one is the simplest: give in to it! Plan the retreat to fit their schedules, not adult ones. Stay up late and get up late. There's no problem with a three o'clock bedtime if things don't start moving until eleven o'clock the next morning. For breakfast, just have juice, milk, coffee, and doughnuts available whenever they get up. If the group is a responsible one, let them plan the schedule with the only given being the number of hours necessary to do the program.

Another help is to schedule "energy releasing activities" throughout the retreat. Contests, dances, games, all are good, but also schedule some more wild activities, such as "A Water Balloon and Shaving Cream Blast" where everyone, including adults, gets involved in a free-for-all. These types of activities are especially helpful early Friday evening. They release tensions and use energy, thus enabling the group to settle down for more serious sessions.

Retreats Are Expensive; How Can You Afford Five in One Year?

It takes some work, but it is possible for any church. First, find inexpensive places to stay. Camps are fine, but also use well-situated private homes or summerhouses and churches if they are available. Camping is inexpensive and would provide a different type of retreat experience. Second, get everyone involved in helping to finance the retreats. Four major sources of funds should be: (1) the church budget, (2) group projects, (3) individual youths, and (4) sponsors who have a special interest in youth.

Does an Emphasis on Retreats Mean No Other Activities in the Youth Program?

Definitely not! But let the group's experience and needs govern what will be done. Don't get locked into thinking that there has to be something going on all the time in order for your church to have a "real" youth program. Remember, one of the main reasons for changing was that continuing activities were not working anymore.

How Can You Possibly Plan Five Meaningful Retreats in Nine Months?

You can't—at least not by yourself. The involvement of others is the key. Let the youth plan as much as they are able (perhaps through a steering committee set up for each retreat). Rely on other adults in the church. They'll be needed as chaperones—so get them in the planning process, too.

If the old way of doing things is getting you and the youth of your church down, then this approach might help turn things around. No program or structure can guarantee success, but trying something new might be the fresh start that youth of your church need. Try it—you just may like it—and so may the youth.

A CHRISTIAN NURSERY CENTER [9]
by Patricia A. Reasoner

The Need

Kevin looked up at his teacher with a radiant smile and said, "Here's a yellow dandelion!" and ran off to the climbing bars at the far end of the playground. On the surface that might not seem to be a very miraculous statement from a four-year-old. But Kevin's life experience was a little out of the ordinary. His journey to a sense of self-worth had really only begun seven months earlier when the board of Christian education of the First Baptist Church of Burlington, Vermont, called a meeting to decide what to do about children often found playing in the church school rooms, wandering through at odd hours, unaccompanied by adults.

It was an impossible task, the board members decided, to determine what to do about these children until more was known about from where the children came, why no parent was looking for them, or what satisfaction it was that they gained by stopping by the church. So, the board members decided to explore the situation for a month to find out these things, while their director of Christian education collected some facts about existing children services already in the area.

Facts go together slowly. Early-childhood programs in the city were few in number and had long waiting lists. The children who played at the church were walked home where families were discovered with preschool children who were not fed adequately. Some were, at the age of two years, unable to use muscles which were

[9] Reprinted from *Baptist Leader*, March, 1974, pp. 5-7.

underdeveloped because the children had been confined. Public school teachers in the congregation discovered children with cigarette burns and bruises from parental abuse. The facts all together said, "The need to help preschoolers is great!" And so, a Christian nursery center was born.

The Purpose

Is it possible to be a community program without giving up the Christian identity? This board felt it was. Keeping in mind the unique value of the Christian community setting and the Christian education objective, they drew up a statement of purpose before they gave any thought to development plans. Very simply it stated:

> To provide a program in Christian education in which a child may grow spiritually and physically; increasing his awareness of life and its relationships; developing healthy feelings about himself and his worth; and building his abilities through experiences related to his size, motor skills, and play interests.

The Association for Childhood Education International provided a *Nursery School Portfolio,* and the denominational presses provided a book entitled *Nursery-Kindergarten Weekday Education in the Church,* both for guidance in the fuller development of a program. The State Department of Education publishes a *Guide for Nursery-Kindergarten Education* and it seemed wise to consult it, for in more and more states there are laws governing weekday childcare programs to which even a church must adhere. It was felt in the Christian nursery center development that this would serve well as a safeguard for children in case of change in leadership of the program, thus letting the law become a trusted friend rather than a threat to this religiously oriented program.

The Staff

Avowedly Christian from its inception, teachers who embodied that life-style were sought. Some of the guidelines for hiring teachers were:

Teacher Qualifications:
1) Exhibits a high degree of spiritual maturity with an ability to express freely her or his Christian faith in a manner understandable to young children;
2) Likes and respects children for what they are;
3) Enjoys working with children and parents;

4) Maintains warm and friendly relationships with children as well as their parents;
5) Is calm, sensitive, and thoughtful of others;
6) Has a genuine sense of humor;
7) Understands how children grow, think, behave, and learn;
8) Values each phase of the child's growth and accepts him or her where he or she is in his or her development;
9) Exhibits teaching capability.

Professional Preparation: LEAD TEACHER... He or she should be a graduate of a four-year college with major work in elementary early childhood education.
ASSISTANT TEACHER... He or she should have had previous experience working with preschool children, preferably in a church school setting. He or she should be over eighteen years of age.

And the guidelines for teacher dismissal were:
... *Mistreatment of a child, verbal or corporal*
... *Inadequacy of instruction*
... *Insubordination or failure to comply with directives*
(no teacher dismissed without personal counseling and a probation period)

The Curriculum

Growing out of the statement of purpose, the curriculum for the nursery center included physical activity (games, rhythms, climbing, balancing, riding); experiences with music, art, and other creative materials, stories, poems, plants, and pets; opportunities for the child to make things at his or her own level of ability, to use his or her own imagination, to solve problems, to grow in independence and self-reliance; opportunities to share experiences, to get along with others; opportunities for some training in habits of eating, resting, dressing, toileting, and washing; science, language arts, numbers, social development, and other related areas. The primary emphasis became the social development of the child with academic preparations provided only for the child who would seek it out himself or herself.

Remember Kevin with the dandelion? Seven months before, when Kevin came to the Center, he was a quiet, detached, uncommunicative child who wasn't even in touch with his mother, the only parent in his life. At four years of age, he lived in a home that included one older brother who was an educable retardee, a younger sister who was openly hostile, a little brother who was the happy baby of the family, and a mother recently separated from her husband and prone to deep depressive states that often resulted in anguished physical abuse of her children. At the end of one term in the life-giving structure of the Christian nursery center, Kevin was secure enough to smile at strangers and trust those in his Center community with his verbalized thoughts.

The first criteria of the Christian nursery center, as its basis for operation was developed, was that at least 10 percent of the full enrollment be held open for children of the immediate community who were in need of this experience, but who, for one reason or another, would not be able to pay for their participation. When the Center began operation, the scope of family situations for which children were enrolled in the program covered:

- only child needing experiences with other children
- abused child, physical or mental
- child for whom religious training is desired
- advanced child needing challenge
- child needing human relations preparation before kindergarten
- child with latent speech patterns
- child of working mother

The Value

Kevin spent only two and one-half hours on three days a week at the Center. Many have asked as they considered the usefulness of a nursery center, "When a child lives daily in an oppressive, painful, often disrupted family, what possible good can two and one-half hours a day in any center do?" Well, (1) he or she is removed from the pressures of his or her home environment and its relationships on a regular basis, giving him or her a consistent hope; (2) he or she experiences love, often for the first time, from an adult; (3) he or she is allowed experimentation for discovery of his or her own unique gifts to life—what lies in his or her human being that no one else can duplicate; and (4) he or she is exposed, perhaps for the first time, to a relationship with a living, loving God. Two and one-half hours is enough time for some life alternatives to be experienced, and, while they cannot be measured in terms of actual effectiveness, certainly it should be better to have offered those hours than to have done nothing.

Kevin is a blue-eyed, curly-haired blond. Kim is a smooth, dark-haired Oriental. Chris is a tall, self-possessed Jewish child—and the group multiplies in its diversity while it learns to live in its oneness as humanity. Living together in the Center setting is work in dead earnest for these children as they find support and security in areas of their needs that parents many times cannot see are there. The Christian Nursery Center then becomes an enlarging, enriching life-force in the child.

Christians have a command to love and a commission to share the faith. In the challenge we have to meet the child; we find hope for doing that, in addition to the joys of enabling him or her to discover the secrets that are within him or her. We turn first to the paths of his or her world to see his or her needs; we turn then to the resources of our world to provide the possibility for him or her to meet those needs. We do it gropingly—we do it exploringly—we do it with the conviction that wherever we begin there is always opportunity for changing, for bettering, for growing in the community we will share.

THE LEARNING COMMUNITY [10]
by Phoebe Cadwallader

By Way of Introduction

Early in 1972, Good Shepherd Baptist Church of Lynnwood, Washington, began a "search for space." The search became necessary because the youth rooms had been destroyed by a fire in an old house on the church property. A building committee was formed to struggle with the problem of too few classrooms, and the budget was limited to the insurance settlement resulting from the fire. Needless to say, the funds available could not rebuild a structure, but it was hoped that through remodeling we could solve the space problem.

At this same time, the Christian education committee was involved in a struggle with declining attendance and increasing feedback from children that they did not find church school a good place to be.

[10] Reprinted from *Baptist Leader,* March, 1974, pp. 2, 4.

Basically, adults felt we had a good educational program. We had dedicated teachers, adequate supplies, cheerful surroundings, and the best curriculum we felt we could find; but children showed us in many ways that they weren't excited about the prospect of being in church school. Some became behavior problems, while others conformed, but in the main they didn't particularly enjoy learning or being in church.

Our Search for Space

The church facility consisted of a chapel with two adjoining wings. The entire facility was around eight years old and modern. One wing housed the two church offices and two classrooms. The other had one classroom, a kitchen, restrooms, and a very large multipurpose room. Folding divider doors made this large room into two large classrooms, which meant we had a maximum of nine spaces for classes, including the two offices and the entry. Clearly, this was not adequate for nursery through adult classes.

The committee discussed and studied many possible suggestions for solutions to the problem, including a paper on open classrooms in public schools. Because we did have the large multipurpose room that was capable of handling more classes in an open style, they began to see the open space idea as a possible solution. The First Congregational Church of Everett, Washington, had gone through a study of space and Christian education models and had developed its model in an open style. After meeting with the Everett leadership and seeing its learning community model, the committee concluded that this was an exciting new possibility for us.

The building committee and the Christian education committee studied the learning community philosophy from the Everett church and also *Values for Tomorrow's Children* by John Westerhoff. As a result of this extensive study, the learning community model was decided upon as the best solution for us at that point of time. We knew it would solve the space problem, and we hoped it would fill children's needs better than the classroom style.

Finally a Happy Solution

We begin Sunday mornings at 10:00 o'clock with the entire church community gathered for worship. The feeling is that children need to experience worship with adults and need to feel they are an important part of the church now. Most of us can identify good religious feelings from worship ritual when we were children, and this is extremely important in a child's religious development. The children's story is an important part of the worship. All the children gather up front for the story and present their offerings at this time. After the story, the children and their adult enablers leave. They spend the next hour and a half in the large multipurpose room. The rest of the church community stays for the sermon part of the worship (usually thirty minutes). After worship, there is a break for conversation and coffee before moving to elective classes for junior high through adult.

Our learning community includes children from three to twelve years old (usually sixty to eighty children) and five or six adult enablers. The adults contract for one month in the learning community or until their particular activity is finished. We also have two adults functioning as floaters. They are not involved in any particular activity but are free to respond to any children having difficulty. They often help children resolve conflicts or help those who have a difficult time deciding in what to become involved. Adults enjoy the freedom this style affords them to be with the children for a month and then to be in adult elective classes. Usually there are enough adults so that each one is in the learning community one month a year. Learning centers are scattered around the room, and the children enjoy discovering what there is to do and who is there to help. Adults have a great need to organize, so for a time we were gathering the children together to tell them what was going on where. Then one Sunday we didn't do it, and the light dawned! We had taken away the joy of discovering. There was so much excitement as the children checked out each center and decided for themselves what they wanted to do. Before, they had decided what to do from an explanation and hadn't bothered to check out other alternatives.

Adults are asked to participate in the learning community by showing and sharing something that really excites them. Usually it's something they are skilled with and feel comfortable showing. They're not uptight with a subject they don't know well; usually they're relaxed because they're confident in doing their own thing. It can be a hobby, vocation, sport, art, carpentry, drama, music, animals, tapes or records, story telling, gymnastics, cooking, etc. The focus is on sharing who you are, sharing your faith, and sharing in learning while *being community*. Being community is a life-style—an intentionality toward *being Christian,* the feeling being that if the children *experience* caring, support, love, acceptance, and redemptive helping relationships, they can better understand what it means to be "covenant people" or "Christian." The activity the children and adults participate in is important, but the sharing of life together becomes the main curriculum. The sharing of the value of each person and the importance of each person feeling good about himself and others is central. Appropriate biblical input is made naturally through themes, worship, church holidays, and informal conversation during activities and church life. An attempt is made to study biblical and theological concepts in depth at the junior high age. Some months have specific themes which follow through in activities. One month the theme was creation. We used a relief map of Puget Sound, a creation-ecology wall mural, a balloon/papier-mâché planet mobile, seeds to plant, finger paints with music, felt banners to make, and clay to sculpt. Throughout, the conversations were involved with creation and God's involvement then and now. Bible material was included at appropriate points to help identify an experience.

At Thanksgiving, the children gathered food for neighbors in need; made cornucopias, turkeys, and concrete mushrooms to take home; constructed and studied about the sukkah booth from Old Testament times; made Palestinian houses; baked unleavened bread; made a magazine-paper collage; created a litany, recorded much of it on videotape, then used closed-circuit TV to review what they had done.

In December, the learning community celebrated the life of Jesus by planning and throwing a surprise birthday party for the entire church. At the end of worship that Sunday, all the children ran in and brought an adult to the party. They had baked and decorated cakes, made root beer, staged a manger scene, decorated a tree, made cards and small gifts for those at the party, baked cookies, decorated the room, created a rhythm band accompaniment to a Bible story, and found a great way to share the excitement of God with us.

We see the learning of information as a method rather than a goal. What a person does with the information is critical. Children must have lived long enough and had sufficient experience to be able to make sense out of the information. Information which cannot build on a child's experience is confusing. When a child has an experience and then discovers the words or information that makes sense out of the experience, that is the moment of greatest learning.

The learning community concept attempts to help children experience the love of God and to create a way by which love can be lived in a community of concern. Children are free to create their own curriculum, as it were. They can determine their own experiences and become very active learners, rather than passive observers. They become more responsible in choosing the activities and persons to whom they will relate. They choose what they're ready for and what interests them. Motivation is high and attendance has gone way up, which is another way children are telling us they have good feelings about the learning community and about the church.

We've been involved in this model for one year, and so far it has responded and evolved as needs became known. When change is needed, it will take new form to meet new demands. For now, we're excited about what's happening to adults and children as they progress together in this free, open style. Children relate to so many adults through the learning community that they are very free to go climb on any lap or grab any hand whenever they feel like it. Adults, too, are very free with the children and often wander into the learning community during their break to see what's going on. They move in and out of the learning community with ease, and the open, informal style lends itself to easy sharing without a feeling of interruption. The barriers usually present between adult and children's programs are absent. We feel that we're one large extended family. The church has included children as a part of its life-style, and they take their part as the church now—not as the church of the future.

The language of faith is not necessarily a spoken language. It's a language that says all the activities we do together contain a religious dimension. We're in process—being and becoming right now—everyone is a learner and everyone is a teacher. We are learning community as well as being a community where we learn.

VACATION CHURCH SCHOOL GOES UNDER. . . WATER [11]
by Sandra Ellis-Killian

"Everybody knows Baptists take their immersion seriously, but giving swimming lessons is going too far!" That thought must have crossed the minds of neighborhood people who saw the sign in front of our church announcing our vacation church school. In big, unmistakable letters it advertised—in addition to Bible lessons, crafts, music, and field trips—"Red Cross Swimming Lessons—FREE." But whatever people thought, they rushed to register their kids, and we had a record enrollment. Our swimming lesson offer enabled us to win a way into many homes which were otherwise indifferent or unreceptive to the church and its message.

Following our VCS of the year before, I made notes of ideas for the

[11] Reprinted from *Baptist Leader*, May, 1977, pp. 54-56.

next year's program. I had a WSI, which is the Red Cross "Water Safety Instructor" certification. It seemed to me that there must be some way to turn that, and my experience teaching swimming, to good use in the church I was serving. At Abington Baptist Church, we needed very much to make some inroads into the community around our church. The way into a home, I had discovered, is through the children. Free swimming instruction under Red Cross certification certainly ought to attract parents, and it did. The swimming program served its purpose well as a selling point. It brought children into a strong Christian education program and brought many families into contact with our church. The summer children's program helped build a reputation for us which has since opened many doors. Of course, quite aside from its promotional value, the swimming lessons met a real community need. We taught swimming skills and water safety principles to children who might not have had the opportunity to learn them for financial or other reasons. What's more, the pool setting gave us each day a unique backdrop to reinforce vividly some of the Bible lessons from vacation church school.

If our church could do it, yours probably can too. Here's how we made it work at Abington Baptist Church.

First, we made sure that our church insurance was adequate for such an undertaking. Next came scouting for a site. A check was made with local country clubs, the YMCA, schools, and apartment complexes. We finally secured the use of two in-ground pools at private homes. Our hosts were told that the use of their pools was a good partnership with Abington Baptist Church to provide a great service to the children and the community. Letters went out to them from our insurance agent informing them of our coverage in order to relieve them of any worries about liability.

In order to staff the program, I taught a Senior Lifesaving course after school hours for two weeks in the spring. Our youth were glad for the chance to earn Red Cross certification which would give them desirable summer jobs and were also glad to lifeguard our VCS swimming (two hours a day for nine days) in return. We were fortunate to have a diving coach in our senior high group who volunteered her services. Six lifeguards and two instructors made up the swim staff. Probably there are one or two persons with WSIs in your congregation. If their certification has expired, pack them off to your local Red Cross for a refresher course, given free of charge. Then you'll have personnel who can train and certify the lifeguards you need. We notified our chapter of the Red Cross of our plans so that it could have on hand all the materials and forms we would need.

Set a ceiling for swimming class enrollments. It was important that no more children be accepted than we could safely accommodate. Kids were signed up on a first-come-first-served basis, and registration was closed when we reached our limit. Parents who were disappointed will be at the head of the line next year, and they appreciated our insistence on safety standards.

We've obtained good free publicity by typing news releases which were sent, often accompanied by black and white glossies, to local newspapers. Flyers, registration forms, and week-before reminders were mailed to community homes.

Kindergartners through junior highs who were enrolled in our morning vacation church school had the option of registering for the swimming lessons in the afternoon. Although we had a nursery class also, we did not have the staff to manage swimming lessons for children that young. (They did, however, enjoy a plastic wading pool in the morning.)

Parents of kids enrolling for swimming lessons were given an "Information Sheet":
  describing the program,
    listing some rules,
      telling them what the children needed to bring,
        saying what to do in case of rain,
          and telling them where to pick children up at the
            end of the day.

A parent also had to sign a prepared permission slip for each child who participated in the swimming classes. We made it clear that swimming lessons were not offered independently of our regular vacation church school morning session. It was tactfully explained, if the question was asked, that swimming lessons were part of a total Christian education project—a vacation church school package deal—and that if we were to fill the swimming classes first, kids who then enrolled in vacation church school couldn't take swimming if they chose. Such a firm policy prevents exploitation of this kind of program and keeps it what we intended it to be: a means of gathering an audience for communicating the Good News. The swimming instruction itself was a splendid and worthy, though only secondary, objective.

To simplify transportation for parents, the swimmers stayed straight through the day, from 9 A.M. until 3 P.M. Our morning session ran from nine until noon. Nursery children and others who were not taking swimming lessons were picked up then, while swimmers changed clothes in the rest rooms and assembled for swimming class roll call. They brought their lunch; the beverages were provided by the church. One or two VCS teachers stayed on to help the swim staff with transportation.

As the swimmers finished eating, they gathered round for a story before going to the pools. Each day I selected some Bible story or event centered upon water: Jonah, stories about the Sea of Galilee, or Jesus' baptism, for example. We discussed the meanings of the two Christian symbols, the fish and the ship. On one occasion, the kids were taken into the baptistry where they heard a description of the ordinance of baptism. For the benefit of the many children from other denominations, we explained why Baptists immerse and why we do not baptize infants. Perhaps it seems gimmicky and contrived to relate Christian teaching to water play. It is. But the fact is that learning and remembering take place through association; so we took full advantage of the opportunity presented to us by making points which could be underscored and recalled by the activity of the moment. It was gratifying (and most entertaining) to watch the kids enact some of the water stories at the pools and to hear them shout out such gems of wisdom as "Hey, look at me! I'm an ichthus!" Swimming from now on will remind many of them of these Bible stories. Few of them, I suspect, will fail to associate fish with the Christian symbol of "Jesus Christ, God's Son, Savior."

Swim time ran from 1 P.M. until 3 P.M., giving us time enough for group and individual instruction as well as for free play. Beginner, Advanced Beginner, Intermediate, and Swimmer classes were taught according to Red Cross specifications. All Beginners were assigned to one pool; we expected that class to the the largest. The prediction came true; there were as many in the Beginner class as in the other three combined, fifty-seven enrolled in all. Classes were taught by rotation, and because we had two hours per day for nine days and an adequate staff, we were able to cover the required material and give enough individual attention to graduate a large number of the children. They were, of course, very proud of their achievements. They received a card recording their swimming achievements. The cards were given privately or mailed so that children who progressed but couldn't meet all the requirements to pass wouldn't have to feel as though they had failed.

The squeals of delight in a cold water splash, the smiles of pride in their new accomplishments, and the gratitude of the parents were the *un*anticipated rewards. It was hard work, and planning had to begin months ahead, but it was such a good experience that we would encourage your next vacation church school to take the plunge!

LOCAL CHURCH CAMPING [12]

The Lynhurst Baptist Church in Indianapolis, Indiana, has had a tradition for a number of years to sponsor and support church camping as a part of its annual church program. A letter from the pastor, Ronald Ricketts, says: "We plan for camping on an annual basis. Our church constitution places the responsibility of our camp upon the Board of Christian Education. We *approach* our time of camping with the philosophy that we can see God in nature and we need to learn to live together as Christian people. Over the years, we have witnessed young people coming to Christ for the first time, others finding a need to seek God's guidance in life, and young and old alike getting to know one another better. Based on these experiences, we conclude that our philosophy is sound and our efforts worthwhile.

"The Board of Christian Education appoints a Camp Director who in turn establishes a Steering Committee to include the Director, Assistant Director, Chief Cook, Program Director, Pastor, and a member of the Board of Christian Education.

"The Steering Committee is responsible to select a camp site, establish adult leadership, determine what activities will be included in the schedule. This committee accepts the total responsibility of the camp, including the menu, selection of curriculum, finances, transportation, and health care.

"The adult leadership is selected from our own congregation. The camp program is set up to provide for three groups of young people: 4th through 6th grades, 7th and 8th grades, and 9th grade through 12th. Sufficient numbers of adult leaders are assigned to each group. These leaders serve as cabin counselors, Bible teachers, and activity leaders, i.e.—for recreation, crafts, etc.

"The church budget provides a specific amount to help cover the expenses of the camp. Each camper is required to pay part of the expenses."

---

[12] Reprinted from a letter received by the author in response to a request for descriptions of "new models" which appeared in *Input*, December 26, 1974.

STUDY TOURS[3]
by Ronald L. Kerr

Our "study tours" have been primarily connected with our senior high group. These have been of two types: (1) long major trips and (2) very short trips.

The short trips have been to the following places: (1) a Jewish Synagogue's Bar-Mitzvah service, (2) a Roman Catholic Mass, and (3) Southern Baptist Theological Seminary's Museum (several times each place). All of these trips involve meeting with the leadership of the place visited for instruction and conversation.

The major trips are taken approximately every two summers. Our first was a trip to Keams Canyon in Arizona to work with the Navajo Indians. We taught Vacation Bible School at two different locations on the Reservation. We have since taken trips to live and work in a black ghetto for a week in St. Louis, working with children and youth. We visited several of our mission stations in Kansas and Oklahoma. On this latter tour to the West, we visited a Spanish-speaking church in Kansas City; Bethel Neighborhood Center in Kansas City; Ottawa University; the mission work at Anadarko, Oklahoma; and Bacone College in Oklahoma. Our text for this particular trip was Acts 1:1. And the theme was that as Acts shows what Jesus continued "to do and to teach" through the apostles, so we were witnessing what Christ continues to do and to teach through those in various locations of our American Baptist Work.

Our last major trip was to Green Lake for a week. This was not a youth conference. We worked for the American Baptist Assembly during the morning hours, had recreation in the afternoon, and studied at night. We used the book of Philippians and the concepts of Transactional Analysis. This last trip was as worthwhile to us as the mission trips we have taken.

We raise our money for these trips a full year in advance. We use methods such as collecting empty pop bottles; having a tree at Christmastime without leaves on it, upon which the members of the congregation place their dollars, pinning them on as leaves of the tree, as special offering. Also, we charge a certain fee to each person going when he or she registers. We feel the fee is a very important part of this for it makes each person take the trip seriously.

The increasing number of students going to summer school, the increase of costs, and other situations are making it more difficult to

[13] Reprinted from a letter received by the author in response to a request for descriptions of "new models" which appeared in *Input,* December 26, 1974.

plan these trips. However, we feel that they are an important way of letting youth experience and study the various mission work of our denominations, and we intend to continue with them.

When we are making trips involving more than one day of driving, I write various pastors along the route and ask them to house all of us in private homes so that we can have a good night of sleep. They are asked also to provide our breakfast for the following morning. This reduces expenses of the trip tremendously. I have never been refused that particular help.

Be assured there is MUCH correspondence necessary for such a trip, and I would consider ten months a MINIMUM of preparation time for a major trip.

Examples of Preparation

Meeting with the young people who are going and with their parents is a part of the preparation. Here is a schedule of meetings in preparation for a trip:

Saturday, June 1, 1:30 P.M. at the church
Saturday, June 8, 1:30 P.M. at the church
Sunday, June 9, 7:00 P.M. at the church

Lesson plans should be completed by the June 8 meeting. (These are plans for the Vacation Church School sessions the young people conducted.) Adults and youth alike will meet on June 9 for a final "talk-through" of the trip.

Also, at the June 1 meeting, several items of information will be given to you: our trip schedule, what to take, etc. (those not able to meet on *any* of these occasions should let me know!).

THESE MEETINGS WILL BE VERY IMPORTANT FOR YOU!!

TRIPPING WITH YOUNG PEOPLE[14]
by John H. McCulley

Need to Be Met

Although we have church school classes for youth and Baptist Youth Fellowship weekly, we have discovered that it is difficult to maintain continuity and to develop anything in depth. Sporadic attendance becomes a problem. There was need to augment these study opportunities.

---

[14] Reprinted from a letter received by the author in response to a request for descriptions of "new models" which appeared in *Input*, December 26, 1974.

Ours is a small church (140 resident members) in a small town (5,000 population). We work to combat parochialism. Overall, there is very little support for our young people, and the generation gap is very evident.

In June, 1973, we traveled to Bacone, making the trip in two days. We rented a nine-passenger station wagon and a U-Haul trailer. We took our own food for the trip.

We made arrangements with the First Baptist Church of Mattoon, Illinois, to sleep there overnight and to use their kitchen, both going out and coming back. The church had been chosen on the basis of its location, but it was also a good choice in terms of facilities. A gymnasium was used to work out kinks resulting from extremely cramped traveling conditions, and showers were available to make closeness more bearable.

At Bacone, we helped a retired couple living at the college to move; cleaned the museum; and painted classrooms, offices, and other rooms. While there, we talked with Indian students, and learned about their situation and their reactions to their situation. There was also time for sightseeing and recreation during the six days we were there. Including the four days for travel, our trip covered ten days.

Building on our experiences at Bacone and desiring to achieve greater results, we began to plan for 1974. It was decided to shift our emphasis and to make this a study-seminar. We would visit and study the church ministering in a metropolitan area in order to enable the young people to see beyond the limitations of their small experience.

We decided to concentrate on Philadelphia because of the many new forms of ministry there. We spent two days in New York City also. Along with the ministries to be visited, there were cultural, historical, and other places of interest to the young people.

In preparation for the trip we chose the theme "How Do You Measure the Church?" Using creative methods, we began a study of the book of Acts in our youth meetings. Time was also allotted for group-building exercises. These exercises and the Bible study were continued during the trip in the evenings in conjunction with an evaluation of the day's events.

Purpose of Trip

The main objective of the trip was to observe the church ministering in the urban area, but there was ample time for recreation and sightseeing.

Each year, the young people have raised the money for their trip by selling articles at a Christmas store, washing cars, sponsoring bake sales, etc. The only requirement for going on the trip is participation in the activities to raise money. This also permits anyone to go regardless of his or her family's financial situation.

Trips of this nature require a great deal of preparation beforehand. The actual trip requires an extended period of time and is quite exhausting for the leaders and participants. However, we believe that the benefits are worth the time and efforts.

The Outcomes of the Trips

1. Experiential learning is more vivid and vital than mere discussion.
2. There is opportunity to develop a wider vision and greater understanding which often eliminates a parochial outlook.
3. A greater number of hours are available for teaching than in the normal weekly one-hour program even though it extends over the year. Regular weekly attendance of the participants is often difficult to maintain in our mobile society.
4. There is opportunity for more continuity without the intervention of time between weekly sessions or frequent absences.
5. There is opportunity to develop deeper relationships between leaders and young people and among the young people.
6. An added dimension is given to regular programming because of the preparation necessary.

This has been neither a cure-all for our youth problems nor a success in reaching all the young people, but it has enriched and enhanced our youth program greatly.

Models for New Groupings of People

AN INTERGENERATIONAL SUNDAY CHURCH SCHOOL [15]
by JoAnn Gilmour

What happened at St. Paul's when children (as young as eight years old) and adults (as young as fifty years old!) became classmates in a Sunday church school program?

There were joys: I like all the different ages together (child); all of our family is coming to church (parent); it is worth it for the time at home when our family is responsible for preparing a lesson (parent); the need for careful planning has produced some ingenious programs (adult); we don't get told what to do, we can help decide (child).

There were growing pains: just trying to become a "group,"

[15] Reprinted from *Baptist Leader,* August, 1975, pp. 13-15.

designing one's own curriculum, searching for resources, listening to one another as persons (regardless of age), providing for a variety of learning activities (not just talking), sharing leadership responsibilities (not just one "teacher").

Three years ago, St. Paul's United Methodist Church in Ithaca, New York, felt the need for a burst of enthusiasm in its ministry with children, youth, and adults at the traditional Sunday morning church school hour. We needed more adults concerned with leadership in the Sunday church school; we needed regular attendance on the part of children and youth; and we needed more "whole families" coming to church together.

At that time, we read about "experiments" in intergenerational groups; we learned about the "Family Cluster Plan" initiated by Dr. Margaret Sawin in Rochester, New York; and we thought about what educators have told us to be true:

> One of the strongest and most viable claims that can be made for the local parish church is that of all our institutions it alone brings together in one fellowship persons of various ages and circumstances so that all together in community can support and affirm the life of each as he endures and negotiates the stress of his own stage of development (William Boyd Grove in *The Church School,* April, 1971).

In September, 1972, 125 persons in groups of twenty-five each began an intergenerational learning experience at our Sunday church school hour. A typical group was made up of five sets of parents, one single adult, two third graders, one fourth grader, one fifth grader, two sixth graders, two eighth graders, and three youth in senior high school. We chose third graders as the youngest to be included because of their growing ability to read and participate in discussions. Within each intergenerational group, we tried to match families by the ages of their children so there would always be more than one young child or one youth of junior high school age.

Families with enthusiasm for the new program and with some leadership skills were recruited to "convene" the groups. The term "convener" (not teacher) was chosen because it was agreed that in intergenerational groups everyone would be involved in establishing goals, deciding on curriculum resources, and, in turn, assuming leadership roles. Assistance in planning for a learning experience and finding resource materials was given by the church's associate pastor and director of Christian education.

We found few units of study designed for use in intergenerational groups. We searched through descriptions of printed curriculum, audiovisual resources, and read every article we could find on intergenerational groups. A list of available resources was compiled for conveners. The list includes denominational curriculum (for grades 5–6 and older), biblical simulation games and simulated activities (such as "Biblical Society in Jesus' Time" written for fourth graders through adults by Jack Schaupp and Donald Griggs), cassette recordings (such as "Repeat the Sounding Joy," The Graded Press, "Faith Alive" series by Thesis), and *The Church School* magazine (the second and third months of each quarter contain undated units of study written for families).

Perhaps outlining two sessions of a unit written by our Associate Pastor Richard McCaughey will give you an idea of planning lessons for intergenerational groups.

An Intergenerational Study of the Exodus Event:
1. The burning bush and Moses' unwillingness to respond to the call of God (Exodus 1–4).
    Two basic themes: that God calls his people (God the initiator) and that the response to the call is not great joy and thanksgiving. Make directives from God to various age groups:
    Children—"Be nice to that kid in school who picks on you."
    Teens—"Be friendly with that person in school everyone labels as odd."
    Adults—"Drop what you are doing and help the migrants in the South."
    Write down in cartoon style how you would argue with God against doing these things.
    Have someone play God and say these directives to the age groups for their responses.
    Talk directly about the story of the burning bush.
2. God's dealings with Pharaoh and the meaning of Passover (Exodus 5:1–13:16).
    Basic theme: God is vengeful to those who stand in his way, and he protects his chosen.
    Divide into two groups. Make one group "suffer" (stand on one foot, clean the room, wash windows, say nothing). Then, give refreshments to the other group. Discuss reactions of both groups. Talk directly about the plagues and Passover. Sing "Let My People Go."

Lesson material for intergenerational groups also includes: celebrating birthdays, anniversaries, graduations, death; responding to illness and loneliness; feasting together at breakfasts and picnics; and visiting residents of nearby homes for elderly persons and leading them in services of worship.

Ninety people are involved in intergenerational groups in this, our third year. Based on our experiences with intergenerational groups in the Sunday church school, here are some observations:

1. A higher degree of commitment to the Sunday church school program exists among families involved in intergenerational groups than among families bringing or sending their children to age-level church school classes; it seems that families in intergenerational groups have a greater sense of being needed by and needing and wanting to be regular participants in their church school groups.
2. Having whole families present in a church school group facilitates developing a caring community: families are spending time with each other, with other families, with single adults, and occasionally with "others to whom they go in Christian ministry" (time they would not usually schedule on their own initiative).
3. Some adults feel uncomfortable with the kinds of learning activities meaningful to children in the elementary grades; it is necessary that the adult try to find meaning in the activity rather than sit back and take an attitude of "letting the children have their time to play because they can't sit still and always discuss the issue the way I can"; for adults it is a revelation to discover that most "learning to be a Christian" happens through other means than the lecture and discussion methods.
4. Having one's family present is conducive to a more honest sharing of one's self, thinking, ideas, dreams; to grow in the Christian faith is to question each other, to search together for truth, and finally to answer one's own questions.
5. When there is no ready-made curriculum, a great deal of time and effort must be given to planning lessons on the part of church staff and those in leadership roles within the group (this is a call for HELP from denominational curriculum writers!).
6. Children, youth, and adults are developing leadership skills as they accept responsibility for the church's ministry through education.
7. The space where groups meet must provide for "getting up and moving around" so that a variety of activities can be used in the learning process.

8. Children, youth, and adults need peer group learning and fellowship activities in addition to the intergenerational group experience.

St. Paul's says "Yes!" to the intergenerational way of learning in the church's program of Christian education.

A FAMILY CLUSTER EXPERIENCE[16]
by Susan S. Bingham

Special times in the church year or the summertime can provide the catalyst for innovative and out-of-the-ordinary church school experiences. The uniqueness of the pre-Easter or pre-Christmas periods lends itself particularly to nontraditional approaches to curriculum. Likewise, the dynamics of lesser numbers, lack of constancy in class makeup because of vacations, and just the general slower pace which is characteristic of summer days and holidays present a unique situation for church school administrators and teachers. The Family Cluster (intergenerational grouping) can emerge as an exceptional experience for almost any Sunday church school and, by its very nature, can meet the requirements of a short-term curriculum need. This is not to say that Family Clusters could not be a more permanent aspect of church school curriculum. If your church school is seeking a fresh route to some new and rewarding experiences surrounding the Savior's birth or resurrection, or if your school needs a summer change, why not approach curriculum, in its complete meaning, in a totally new fashion? The church school of First Baptist Church, Ypsilanti, Michigan, did just this by means of Family Clusters.

Some of the members of the board of Christian education had envisioned the possibility of using the Family Cluster approach as an alternate curriculum experience "sometime." As the need for a unique summer program developed last year, it was decided to use the Family Cluster idea for our church school. Basic to the interest in Family Clusters was the belief of many that there has been in our highly mobile society a loss of important interaction between the generations. In the years since World War II when the nuclear family concept has grown and intensified, grandparents have found themselves separated from the lives of their children and grandchildren and vice versa. Also, some board members were aware that researchers studying family dynamics have been rediscovering some of the advantages inherent in close intergenerational relationships.

[16] Reprinted from *Baptist Leader,* February, 1977, pp. 14-15.

The Summer Curriculum Committee, appointed by the board of Christian education, then met, with the objective of determining the manner in which the Family Cluster Program would be developed and implemented. A brainstorming technique resulted in several things:
1. *The Setting of Objectives*
   a. to develop a viable summer program and not just a stopgap measure, as in many other years.
   b. (affective domain) to foster a sense of family both within families and between families of the church.
2. *Determination of a Theme*
   "The Parables of Jesus" was the theme selected. Each Cluster was to choose its own parable and develop it for presentation in any manner it chose. Using the talents of all ages and encouraging intragroup relationships were primary Cluster objectives.
3. *Method of Publicity*
   It was decided to print a brochure explaining the Family Cluster concept, theme of the program, and time schedules. A perforated section was included for registration purposes. Other publicity was given through the weekly newsletter, and spot announcements were made in the Sunday bulletins.
4. *Planning of a Sharing Experience*
   A strategy was developed whereby Clusters would share their parables with the church school at the close of the summer.

About fifty persons indicated an interest in the Family Clusters. There were families of three to five people as well as single-member families. Children from ages four and five, as well as grandparents—sometimes all within one family—had registered for the program. In order to keep groups approximately the same size, the Summer Curriculum Committee decided to group persons arbitrarily in clusters, giving them the option of choosing the parable they wished. A list of the parables of Jesus had been prepared by the committee, and this sheet was circulated among the Clusters. Another method would be to let persons gather as a total group and move into groups formed on the basis of interest. In this instance, common interest in a parable would set the limits of the group. (Perhaps it should be pointed out here that during this time traditional classes on adult, youth, and children's levels were also maintained for those who preferred that method. Many, whose attendance was to be sporadic, chose these traditional classes.)

Three groups of fifteen to seventeen persons were formed. Families were always kept intact as a basic element in the Family Cluster experience. Two or three families were represented by three generations. It was hoped that the church family concept was experienced by all participants.

Parables chosen were as follows, with a brief description of how they were developed:

1. *The Parable of the Rich Man and Lazarus* (Luke 16:19-31). One of the Clusters decided to dramatize this familiar story. Some of the adults collaborated to write a skit. One of the teenagers wrote some original music for different instruments, and the youth of the group provided the musical background for the play. The small children were guided by a kindergarten teacher in the group in preparing murals to be used as backdrops in the skit's presentation. The talents of all were utilized, and a real sense of family existed.

2. *The Parable of the Talents* (Matthew 25:14-30). Members of this Cluster moved out-of-doors for most of their meetings. They decided to illustrate this parable with a slide presentation; after initial planning, they met in the garden belonging to one of the families in that Cluster. An inexpensive Kodak camera recorded the story of the talents as told by Jesus. Participants—children and adults—garbed in first-century dress dramatized the parable and gave the story a modern-day application by showing how twentieth-century Christians can use their talents for Christ and the church.

3. *The Parable of the Wise and Foolish Virgins* (Matthew 25:1-13). One Cluster developed this parable by acting out the story in pantomime. A narrator accompanied those persons acting out the skit. All ages participated in this aspect of the presentation. Several members of the group formed a chorus which combined voice and instrumental renditions of "Give Me Oil in My Lamp." These were taped and provided the background for the pantomime and narrative.

Perhaps these words written by one of the Cluster leaders best summarize the evaluations after the experience: "... the mechanics of our group ... aren't all that made this a worthwhile experience. It was the spirit which prevailed that made us a family. This I will remember. We were all 'people'—not teenagers, retirees, kids, grown-ups—just people showing our love and respect for each other through discussions and activities together. It was special!"

If Family Clusters were formed to function during the Lenten season, one group could present the Garden of Gethsemane experience, another the drama of the Upper Room, another the events of Palm Sunday, and a fourth group could portray the empty tomb account. Such a journey through the pre-Easter season could lead the participating families of a church, and indeed an entire fellowship, into a unique Easter Sunday experience.

Likewise, the pre-Christmas period could be a time of family sharing through intergenerational groupings. The biblical accounts of the Old Testament prophecies, the shepherds in the fields, the manger story, and the visit of the wise men to the child Jesus could each be developed in exciting ways and shared with the congregation.

Our experience with the Family Cluster was a good one. We plan to use it again next summer using "Family Living" as our theme. The Family Life Education Planning Kit (LS15-315) available through Judson Book Stores will be a main resource. We would recommend the Family Cluster experience to your church!

ADOLESCENTS LOOK AT FAMILY CLUSTERS [17]
by Margaret M. Sawin

What have youth been saying about family clusters—"the church education program with families at its center"?

"My cluster helped me to relate to other adults and to get to know other parents."

"Our cluster is the one set thing in a week which draws our family together."

"I noticed that studying about conflict in the family helped me in my family."

"Religion deals with life, and cluster deals with life."

What Is a Family Weekly Cluster?

These were some of the comments a number of our youth expressed in reaction to being a part of a family cluster this year. The family cluster is a gathering of five or six families. They support each other and are part of an educational experience in which every family member is a full participant.

[17] Reprinted from *Baptist Leader,* February, 1974, pp. 57-63.

Family Cluster Goals

1. To provide an intergenerational group of families where children and youth can easily relate to adults, and adults to children and youth.
2. To provide a group which supports and respects its members.
3. To help parents better understand their children through contact with other children, and, likewise, to help children gain a better insight into their parents through contact with other parents.
4. To provide an opportunity for families to work on issues and topics related to their faith, to themselves as individuals, and to their family life.
5. To provide an opportunity for families to model and share their own family's style of decision making, disciplining, interrelating, problem solving, etc.
6. To provide an experience where adults share their concerns regarding the meaning of life's experiences amidst a time of rapid social change and aberration of traditional values, and where youth can deal existentially with their world experiences and check them out in a supporting group of other youth and adults.

Experience Teaching

To further these goals, a model of experiential education is used. Members of the cluster have an experience together and then discuss the experience. Experiences include: simulation games, role playings, finger paintings, clay modelings, story tellings, creative writings, collages. With this approach, young children can participate and learn from an emotional response, while other children and adults can participate and learn from a cognitive response.

Family Contract

Children and teenagers agree to a family contract whereby each member of the family contracts to be in a cluster for a certain number of weeks. The cluster contract of the families as a group also assures that teenagers, as well as children, have a voice in cluster affairs and are heard. They know that they are an important part of the group, and they respond in a responsible way.

Fifteen youth from two clusters of the First Baptist Church of Rochester, New York, were interviewed about their feelings from being in a cluster and the kinds of experiences they saw as valuable through membership in such a group. The age spread of adolescents was one twelve-year-old, six thirteen-year-olds, one fourteen-year-old, three fifteen-year-olds, and four sixteen-year-olds. The interviewed group was composed of six girls and nine boys. Most of the adolescents had been in a cluster two years. One of the healthy points of cluster is that all children and youth like to be present and enjoy the general format. They form an intergenerational peer group that can play, joke, and interact with each other.

Youth and Adult Friends

Adolescents felt that one of the greatest assets the cluster experience brought was helping them to become sincere friends with numerous adults and to be taken seriously by them. In our culture, there are few places where adolescents meet a number of adults other than their parents and interact with them for lengthy periods of time. Almost all the teenagers said that when they see a "cluster adult friend" at other functions within the church setting, they don't panic and think, "What am I going to say to this adult?" Rather they consider the adult as another friend with whom they can easily share things in common. To accomplish this, we often divide into pairs or triads within the cluster, allowing for a cross-generational "mix." Another activity is using "simulated families" where the father of one family, mother from a second family, and children from a third are brought together in a "pretend family." This may occur when we are discussing a topic too threatening to handle within their own family setting, or the simulated family may make up a role play to present or do some other activity together.

If the ideas of The White House Conference for Children are correct, then clusters fulfill a function in helping generations mingle more intentionally and seriously:

"We call upon all institutions ... to initate and expand programs that will bring adults back into the lives of children and children back into the lives of adults. This means the reinvolvement of all ages with parents and other adults in common activities and responsibilities."

The Whole Family Together

Family cluster is the one setting where the whole family is together for a learning experience. Many youth indicated that it is often the only activity in which the family participates together during the week. Most church programs are based on the "split-level approach." Children go to one classroom, teenagers to another, and adults someplace else. We believe that parents are the primary teachers of values to their children who, in turn, learn to refine their values by discussing them with other persons. The teenagers also felt that discussion in clusters helped them to understand adult thinking and allowed the opportunity to question and discuss adult ideas and comments. If the church does not provide for adult-youth conversations, we are neglecting an important part of value education for adolescents and adults.

We Came to Like Our Parents . . .

Teenagers also felt that clusters provide an opportunity for them to see how unique their parents really are. It helped them better understand and thereby allow for more tolerance of their parents' personalities and values. The cluster experience helps a family look at itself and perhaps understand facets of its own functioning which may never have been articulated or pointed out. It helps to dispel family myths. It allows both youth and parents to understand the reality of family life and the role of parents. Teenagers are exposed to the realism of parenthood through people other than their own parents. Parents see themselves through the eyes of youth from other families.

Stronger Families

Family clusters also provide an avenue in which families can watch how other families operate, function, and live out their concerns. A family can see how another family interacts and then consider change in their own living because of this new awareness. Such an experience permits teenagers to enlarge their vision about modes of family functioning. It gives them other alternatives to consider in their style of family living.

Multiple-family-therapy research shows that families help each other to change and grow more than the therapist does. Therefore, we assume that families also help each other by being together in a family cluster. Our adolescents seem to think this was true. The act of discussing uniqueness, differences, and their feelings themselves helps them feel closer to each other as family members. *This meets one assumption of the Family Cluster Model: that, in stressing diversity, we often promote more acceptance and thereby closeness and affection among family members.* At a time of lostness, aloneness, alienation, and confusion in our society, it is good to have adolescents who are feeling that their family ties are becoming stronger.

Cluster Curriculum

The specific context of a cluster is developed at the request of families. Our directions in Rochester have included:
—communication within the family
—authority and power in the family
—conflict and its resolution
—beliefs and values
—our sexuality and its importance
—what about grief and death?
—transactional analysis of our interactions
  (based on Eric Berne's theory)

Several teenagers in our interview mentioned that the unit on conflict/resolution changed the way they related to other family members. The unit on beliefs helped them to articulate better what they believed in. A number of them felt that cluster taught them about the importance of personal relationships and, therefore, life in its larger scope. One said: "Religion deals with life, and cluster deals with life in an up-to-date way—so our beliefs and actions often come out of cluster." (To me, this is religious nurturing at its best.) At the same time, however, some adolescents were not aware that cluster learning is religious. They defined "religion" as "something to do with worship in church." They were unable to interpret religion into everyday life. Therefore, unless we can help persons associate their interpretation of religious meanings with their day-to-day behavior, we become "sounding brass or a clanging cymbal." **Religion is a force by which one lives**—not a ritual undertaken once a week. Children and adults need to be exposed to religious ideas daily through their family living. Cluster can serve as a place where this is emphasized.

Cluster Education Is Fun

One aspect of cluster which the youth emphasized was that of having fun. Cluster is a place where they meet friends of all ages, play games, participate in sports activities, and have fun during the meal. They said, "We know there is a fun side to religion; we don't just read the Bible!" They especially liked an all-day planning retreat in the fall and a concluding weekend retreat in the spring. They disliked "stupid" experiences which made no sense to them and also evaluations at the conclusion of study units. **They would have liked the cluster period of two hours per week to have been longer!**

One of the healthy aspects of cluster experience is the family "spin-offs" which happen as a result of having been together. Often a discussion is started in cluster which is continued in the car driving home or later at home. At that time, parents become the "interpreters" to the youth of what has been happening with cluster. This encourages the parent to assume his or her rightful place in the religious nurturing process of his or her child. The Jewish home has kept this process within the family. This has been one of the reasons why the Jewish people have been able to maintain a strong faith identity. When we "loan" out our children to the church school, we are encouraging parents to lose their right as interpreters of the faith. Parents and churches need to work more diligently at helping the process of "family building" within an age of pluralism and mass media.

The First Baptist Church of Rochester has been working with family groups for three years and has provided a model which a large number of churches of all denominations across the country are utilizing. Training in leading a family cluster is available each summer in a number of week-long laboratory schools across the country. Orientation to the concept and training in the use of it are services available to churches through **Family Clustering, Inc., P.O. Box 18074, Rochester, NY 14618.** Dr. Margaret M. Sawin developed the model and is a part of a group of skilled persons who lead such training and provide consultant services.

Alternative Meeting Times

THE GATHERING PLACE [18]
An Intergenerational Ecumenical Adventure
• by Russell C. Petrie

"Wow, what a mouthful!" was the first response to the suggested title for our summer program. The title, "borrowed" from another denomination's curriculum materials, described exactly what we were trying to do—a family-oriented evening ministry shared by Baptist, Episcopal, and Presbyterian churches for one week in late July.

As our board of Christian education looked ahead toward summer, we discovered that leaders who had been available in previous years for day camp, discovery trips, and similar programs would not be able to help this year. We could get leaders, however, if we considered evening rather than daytime activities.

[18] Reprinted from *Baptist Leader,* December, 1976, pp. 7-9.

Also, we felt that a neighborhood ministry could best be done in cooperation with other churches in the community, enriching leaders as well as participants. Representatives of the Presbyterian church across the street and the Episcopal church just four blocks away enthusiastically responded to our invitation to join in planning this "adventure."

The resulting planning group agreed that too often the families who come to church together are divided by ages and that for our "adventure" we would like to be "intergenerational," thereby keeping the family together. The invitation was issued to young and old, single and family units, and the hours were set for 7:00 to 8:30 P.M. in order to include younger children. When registration was complete, we divided the entire group into "families" for the week. Each natural family was the core to which we added a few individuals who came alone; thus, we worked as an extended family—with grandparents, aunts, uncles, and cousins.

One other guideline in planning was that we wanted to do things not normally done in our churches' Christian education programs. We decided that we would make this week an "adventure" as we tried new activities. Thus we developed our "intergenerational ecumenical adventure" and chose "The Gathering Place" as an appropriate title.

We began on Sunday evening with a picnic in the neighborhood park (complete with a few raindrops at suppertime). The evening included a simulation game, with each "family" taking a "hike" in the mountains and encountering a storm, bad drinking water, sprained ankles, and other problems with which they would have to deal as a family. Comments following the hike indicated that this adventure did serve as an icebreaker and did begin to build a family spirit within the extended group. A picnic supper, singing and games, and a concluding informal worship which was led by a family completed the first evening's adventure.

Attendance proved to be inconsistent during the rest of the week, but each evening started with a "together time" which built on previous experiences and also gave us a common ground for the evening ahead. Those who had missed one evening had no difficulty joining in when they returned the next evening. This period of time in the schedule, which brought us together in "the gathering place," included stories, records, songs, films, and even a bit of church history and theology! The "together time" was time well spent as it directed our thinking toward the evening's theme and explained the choices of activities related to this theme which were available for the evening.

On Monday each family chose an activity which involved all of the family members working together. Some drew murals depicting family experiences, including the experiences of each member of that extended family. Others prepared a collage expressing family feelings, placing them on the sides of large boxes stacked pyramidlike toward the ceiling. (This was a "kiosk," a new word our committee learned in planning together.) A third family group designed a family coat of arms, discussing the family motto and picturing specific ideas about the family.

When the families came together, they entered into discussion, and many positive comments were heard about the evening's experiences. One family group again led in a time of informal worship.

Tuesday was "creative activity" night, with individual choices of methods for making symbols, such as a fish or a cross, of the larger Christian family. The media that were used included woodworking, imitation stained glass, burnt matches, and molded dough (which was then baked and painted). Everyone spent an enjoyable evening expressing his or her creativity.

On Wednesday the choices were again individually made among sharing in drama, choral reading, or creative movement. Each group spent time learning and experiencing that particular activity; they also prepared a short presentation for Thursday night's closing worship.

Thursday evening each family made banners which were then carried on a "walking tour" of the three churches. The pastor of each church spoke briefly about that church's local history and pointed out some distinctions of architecture and furnishings. The week's experience was concluded with a brief worship service in which each family shared, using the creative expression prepared the previous evening. Three or four banners were hung in each church as a continuing reminder to each congregation of "The Gathering Place" experience.

When we evaluated our week together, the positive reactions led us to plan a one-day "Gathering Place" for early November as a Thanksgiving celebration. During the weeks following "The Gathering Place," we exchanged banners among the churches as a renewed reminder of our shared experience. Enthusiasm continues to be high and will undoubtedly lead to another "Gathering Place" next summer.

A SATURDAY CHURCH SCHOOL [19]
by the Reverend Dr. Harold A. Carter

While all over the country people are saying that the church school is dead, New Shiloh Baptist Church in Baltimore has begun what might be called the "rebirth" of the church school. Pastors and churches everywhere are looking for new ways of expressing the love of God for man. New Shiloh has found some answers.

On Saturday, October 13, New Shiloh Baptist Church began what they call the Saturday Church School. The goal of the program is to bring men and women, boys and girls to an awareness of the love of God and the activity of God in the lives of all persons. This goal is to be achieved not only through Bible study but also through subjects related to the affairs of persons. Such subjects include reading, arithmetic, arts and crafts, black history, black literature, home economics, typing, and music.

On opening day, more than five hundreds persons were present. To date, more than 750 persons are registered and are attending. This number includes vast numbers of both adults and young people, all coming to learn. The program makes use of college, high school, grade school, and vocational teachers, as well as generally dedicated Christians to teach and impart both the Bible and remedial skills for all pupils. The program also makes use of a full-time director of Christian education, Mrs. Brenda J. Greene. Among the topics being taught are: God as Father, God in Nature, God's Initiative in Worship, and Man's Response to God.

This program will continue every Saturday until June, from 10:00 A.M. to 12:30 P.M. No registration fee is charged, and all interested persons may attend. It will continue yearly on a September to June basis. The pastor of the church is the Reverend Dr. Harold A. Carter, and the church is located in the heart of the inner city at Fremont Avenue and Lanvale Street.

"BIG TUESDAY" [20]
by Joseph D. Huse

For the last two years, our board of Christian education has been experimenting with alternatives to the traditional vacation church school. Our first major break with the established pattern was our

---
[19] Reprinted from *Baptist Leader,* August, 1974, pp. 7-9.
[20] Reprinted from *Baptist Leader,* May, 1975, pp. 53-54.

format two summers ago when we tried a 9 A.M. to 3 P.M. program for five days from Nursery Department through the Junior Department. Our evaluations after that trial experience indicated that young children experienced a kind of "battle fatigue" that worked against the effectiveness of the program. On the other hand, the older children enjoyed the longer sessions, and they greatly benefited from the more relaxed time structure, field trips, and more complex projects that were possible in an all-day program.

On the basis of the first year's experience, we raised the question of whether we could have the "best of both worlds" in our summer program. Our conclusion was that there is no law that says everybody in a vacation school program has to meet at the same time, at the same location, for the identical periods of time. Therefore, our program this year included three major divisions. One was an ecumenical vacation church school for young children for a week in cooperation with two other churches in our city. The Junior Department designed a weekend retreat experience, and the Middler Department engaged in a program which was christened "Big Tuesday."

Big Tuesday was an experience held on six consecutive Tuesdays in June and July. The theme "Co-creators with God" was developed by a five-member leadership team which captured the imagination of both Middler students and parents. If there is a brief way to describe the participation of the learners, it can be summed up in the words "creative involvement." Our attempt was to help the children discover their own creative potential, as well as to help them understand ways in which they are related to and dependent upon others. The context of all we did was under the umbrella concept that God is the author of all of creation.

An introductory comment by one member of the leadership team summed up what we were all about: "We want to look at God's creation and why we are here. We want to see how we help God create and how God helps us." The role of the adults was that of resource persons. The children were the prime focus of the program—not the teachers! When there was something to be learned from Bible study, the children were given the tools, but they did the research. When there were craft projects to be made, the learners constructed them from raw materials—not from prepackaged commercial kits. When we went fishing, they made their own fishing poles from available tree limbs. We did provide hooks and line, but they dug their own worms and fashioned bobbers from walnut shells. The end result was not fancy or professional-looking items that would impress a judge at the local art exhibit, but each project was really their own.

A brief overview of our program will indicate the scope of the series:

The first Big Tuesday focused on study of Genesis 1 and 2; it included a Moody Science film, guided Bible study, construction of a mural illustrating the seven days of creation, and a discussion of the privilege and responsibility of mankind who was given dominion over all of God's creation.

The second Big Tuesday was devoted to listening and responding to music. The children were involved in listening exercises and games; they participated in painting to mood music and expression through creative dance. The project they liked most was making their own musical instruments and creating their own kind of music.

The third Big Tuesday program explored the concept that God provides for our food. The entire day was spent exploring the life cycle of a grain of wheat. A local farmer supplied the wheat which the children planted, winnowed, ground, and ate; they explored harvesting methods from Bible times to the present. They learned how flour was processed and made their own bread. The Bible study included research with a dictionary and concordance to see how grain and bread were referred to in the Bible. A trip to a local grocery helped them discover the variety of products that are dependent upon wheat as an essential ingredient. A craft project concluded the day as the students constructed a wooden plaque that was decorated with seeds, stalks of wheat, and included the bread recipe.

The fourth Big Tuesday featured a trip to our state capital. We went on a guided tour of the state house and three departments of government. We also enjoyed sightseeing in the downtown area of Indianapolis and finished our trip at the zoo.

The fifth Big Tuesday program was spent along a river bank. The nature outing involved cooking over an open fire, fishing, tracking wild animals, making sand candles and plaster of paris casts of animal tracks, shaking down insects, and playing games created from artifacts of nature.

The final Big Tuesday program involved an evaluation and final report, consisting of the production of our own newspaper with a multimedia slide and tape combination that was later shared with the congregation. Part of the day was spent at the local newspaper office, interviewing the editor and observing the production of the evening newspaper.

In addition to the program content, some of the success of the series resulted from the planning, preparation, and promotion of the program. The symbol for the program was a picture of a large elephant with the words "Here's a Big One!" Each student was given a "Big Tuesday Calendar" prior to the program with a page for each day attached, which described the main activities and goals for each session. It was an excellent way to communicate with parents and children alike. The calendar included information for each day, instructing them on:
(1) when to bring a bag lunch,
(2) when spending money was needed,
(3) the hours of each session (the hours varied depending on the activity for the day),
(4) the appropriate clothing to wear.

The program received an excellent reception from children, parents, and leaders. This coming summer holds possibilities of an even richer experience.

A CREATIVE APPROACH TO SCHEDULING IN THE CHURCH[21]
(Are You Ready for Fall?)
by Richard C. Hutchison

Let's face it! Today's individual or family finds it difficult to attend church programs week after week on a year-round basis, or even from September until June as many churches are scheduled. The fact is that a large percentage of the members of most congregations attend on a very irregular basis. The result is that classes, courses, and such programs as are premised on continuity are only minimally effective.

What's to be done about it? Well, we obviously do not want to schedule and plan so as to encourage irregularity! On the other hand, we take an ostrich approach if we assume regularity. The ideal solution is one that provides continuity and flexibility, is meaningful to the person who attends throughout the year, but also offers viable options to those who are unable or unwilling to commit themselves to be present week after week, month after month.

A format being adopted by an increasing number of churches is that of dividing up the church program year into manageable portions. I recently worked with a committee which took this tack in planning.

[21] Reprinted from *Patchwork*, vol. 2, no. 2 (1975), pp. 1-2.

The program year running from September through June was divided into segments which were called "units." A unit was defined as a period including five Sundays. The core of their program was to take place on Sunday mornings and Wednesday evenings.

Of itself, the above is not unusual. However, it was decided that persons would be asked to register or enroll for each unit rather than for the year. Advance publicity will emphasize that attendance throughout a unit is vital if the unit is to be meaningful. Topics, themes, and the major concepts to be dealt with in each unit will be stated well in advance, and families and individuals will enroll in as many as they feel they can attend throughout.

Both Sunday morning and Wednesday evening programs will be planned in five-week segments and together will make up a single unit. The Wednesday programs, however, will not take place each week but will be scheduled during the first and last week of each unit. In other words, a unit will consist of a course which will meet for an hour on each of five consecutive Sundays and for two hours on the first and last Wednesday evenings of that period. That is a total of nine hours of in-class time for each group.

The program year as scheduled on the above basis resulted in a total of seven units from September through May:

Two prior to Thanksgiving
One during Advent
Two after Christmas until Lent
One during Lent
One after Easter through May

Christmas and Easter Sundays were excluded for special celebrations.

Teachers and leaders will be recruited by units, rather than for the entire year. The teaching team responsible for each unit will be accountable for advance planning together and the leading of five Sunday and two Wednesday sessions. A given person could certainly teach more than one unit during the year, and it is hoped many will. However, the plan will give many persons, who can manage a five-week commitment, but who are unable to work for a whole year, the opportunity to teach.

Also, the unit arrangement allows for greater flexibility in planning teaching units correlated to the special seasons of the church year such as Advent and Lent.

The Wednesday programs have been planned to include a meal and to have programs for all ages, including care for very young children.

Thus, entire families will be able to attend. The time block chosen was 5:45 to 8:30 P.M. so younger children would not be kept up late.

A sample schedule is reproduced below. Obviously, each church would need to revise it to its own needs, but it may stimulate your own group to give serious consideration to the "unit" concept.

1975-76 SCHEUDLE

UNIT 1	Sundays: Sept. 21, 28; Oct. 5, 12, 19
	Wednesdays: Sept. 17 & Oct. 15
UNIT 2	Sundays: Oct. 26; Nov. 2, 9, 16, 23
	Wednesdays: Oct. 22 & Nov. 19
UNIT 3	Sundays: Nov. 30; Dec. 7, 14, 21, 28
	Wednesdays: Dec. 3 & 17
UNIT 4	Sundays: Jan. 4, 11, 18, 25; Feb. 1
	Wednesdays: Jan. 7 & 28
UNIT 5	Sundays: Feb. 8, 15, 22, 29; March 1
	Wednesdays: Feb. 4 & March 3
UNIT 6	Sundays: March 14, 21, 28; April 4, 11
	Wednesdays: March 10 & April 7
UNIT 7	Sundays: April 25; May 2, 9, 16, 23
	Wednesdays: April 21 & May 19

WEDNESDAY "UNIT NIGHTS" FORMAT

5:45 P.M.	Supper
6:15—7:15	Youth Choir Rehearsal (Junior, Senior High)
6:15—8:15	Children's classes, Kindergarten to Grade 6
6:30—8:15	Adult Classes or Programs
7:15—8:15	Junior High and Senior High "Rap" Sessions
8:15—8:30	Closing Worship for all

Celebrations/Festivals

FESTIVAL OF FAITH[22]
by Elizabeth J. Loughhead

Knowing what you believe and being able to state your faith are necessary and basic requirements for every Christian. Certainty about faith and belief is prerequisite to a church's renewal. Clarity

---

[22] Reprinted from *Baptist Leader,* May, 1977, pp. 50-52.

about faith issues encourages informed worship experiences, enables intelligent witness to others, and results in enthusiastic church membership and mission in the world. These were the arguments presented by the pastor of Calvary Baptist Church of Denver, Colorado, as he sought to lead the congregation toward a renewing experience. As a part of the renewal emphasis, the congregation participated in a Festival of Faith. For seven weeks, faith issues were the focus for Sunday morning worship. The sermon dealt with an issue each week. Music, Scripture, and litanies all contributed to an understanding of the topic for the day. A character out of our Baptist heritage appeared during worship and spoke of her or his faith journey and the resulting contribution to Baptist belief. A Sunday evening talk-back session allowed those interested in the issue of the week to dialogue in greater depth with the preacher and with each other. As a part of the festival, each church school class was asked to prepare an affirmation of faith, its members hammering out together what they believed and stating it in clear terms.

The team of teachers working with the juniors wondered how the Festival of Faith could be a good learning experience for the children of their classes. There was no question that fifth and sixth graders needed to know what they believed, and that they would grow in their understanding as they tried to put their faith into words. Many of the children in the class were already members of the church, and others would soon be attending Pastor's Class and preparing for baptism. Junior children at Calvary are present in morning worship and would hear the sermons and the testimonies of the persons out of our Baptist history. Listening to the life stories of Roger Williams, Isaac Backus, Ann Judson, Walter Rauschenbusch, Helen Barrett Montgomery, Martin Luther King, Jr., and Harry Emerson Fosdick could inspire them to live a similar life of faith and witness. Class discussion could provide talk-back sessions for the children at their own level. The junior teaching team decided to help their class become a cooperative part of the Festival of Faith.

Several weeks into the festival, the junior class began to work on its affirmation of faith. Each week, the children were told what the topic would be for the next Sunday. For example, the first week the children were told to consider what they believed about God. They were asked to think about it during the week and to come prepared to write their ideas down on paper. Upon arriving the next Sunday, each child was given a card and told to finish the sentence "I believe that God is...." The sentence was to be completed with each child's ideas expressed in her or his own words. All the ideas were considered, unclear meanings were clarified, and similar thoughts were combined. Much care was taken not to change the words of the children and to include all thoughts and ideas. A final paragraph was prepared for inclusion in the statement of faith. This process was repeated for each of the faith topics: God, Jesus Christ, humanity, salvation, and the world. At the end of several weeks, the following affirmation of faith was completed by the juniors:

WE BELIEVE THAT:
God is loving, caring, and forgiving because God is love. God is the only God there is and is the Creator of all the world and the whole universe. God is really alive and is Someone to talk to, always listening, always there, and always understanding your feelings. If you listen to God in return, you will find happiness and wisdom for your life.

WE BELIEVE THAT:
Jesus is God's Son, sent to show us what God wants us to do. He is God's Good News. Jesus is also the greatest man who ever lived. He is loving, caring, and understanding, just as God is. Jesus is alive NOW, and in him we find our hope to do right tomorrow.

WE BELIEVE THAT:
People are God's children created to be receptive to God's way for them. They are capable of loving and of living together as friends, making the world a better place. However, people are not perfect. They are often mean to each other. They are sometimes dumb and jumpy and think too much about money. People need to worship God and ask for forgiveness.

WE BELIEVE THAT:
The world is God's creation given to us to enjoy. It is not ours alone but is for all people. Since it is God's creation, it is to be cared for and not killed off by our selfish use of it. Although the world sometimes seems crazy and mixed-up, it is an exciting place to live. Because God and Jesus are here, love is here, and our world can be full of love.

The children were pleased with the results and were glad to be able to share their affirmation with their parents and friends during a program presented to summarize their semester's work. The teachers and ministerial staff were delighted with the obvious thought the children had put into their statements. The pastor used portions of the affirmation in responsive readings during morning worship.

The Festival of Faith culminated in an Arts Festival. Church school classes were asked to prepare a visual representation of their faith statements. Individuals also were encouraged to create contributions for the Arts Festival through writing, painting, sculpturing, composing, or other media of expression. These were to be based on their faith and belief. Junior class learners and teachers brainstormed how they might present their affirmation in an artistic manner. Since it was the bicentennial year and colonial days were being highlighted everywhere, the class decided to prepare a large sampler done on white burlap with cross-stitch and other stitchery patterns, using red and blue yarn. Boys in the class who would never consent to "sewing" were glad to do "stitchery" and proved to be among the best workers on the sampler. Symbols of some of the ideas in the statement were created out of felt and were added to the sampler. A frame of wood, painted bright red, completed the project; and the juniors' contribution to the Arts Festival was hung proudly in the front of the sanctuary.

Several members of the class wrote poems and stories for the magazine of creative writings. Others had paintings on display in the art gallery in the foyer of the church. One boy wrote the words and music to an original hymn which was sung by the senior choir as an anthem in public worship.

The Festival of Faith was a good learning experience for the junior children. Learners and teachers together grew in their understanding of the faith and in their ability to articulate their own beliefs. The children were proud to be a cooperating and contributing part of their church. It was for all a *festival* of faith. Much was found in the faith for which to hold a festival.

CELEBRATING PENTECOST [23]
by Virginia G. Leonard

What is Pentecost? It is the birthday of the church, the day the Holy Spirit came to the disciples, the day three thousand persons were baptized.

How can we celebrate it today? We can celebrate with a party, with sharing the joy and oneness the Spirit gives the church, with baptisms.

[23] Reprinted from *Baptist Leader,* May, 1977, pp. 5-7.

These are only some of the possible answers to these two questions. Each Christian and each church must find personal answers just as each of us must make faith itself personal. But discovery and self-discovery can be aided by knowing the experience of others. I want to share with you what Pentecost has come to mean to me and to the church with which I have celebrated it.

Pentecost Is the Bible Story

Jesus telling his disciples, "John baptized with water, but before many days you shall be baptized with the Holy Spirit" (Acts 1:5).

The disciples meeting together, praying, struggling to understand all that had happened to Jesus, seeking to discover what he expected from them.

The disciples, stirred by a wind that filled the house, seeing tongues of flame resting on each person, uttering ecstatic speech.

Peter, the disciple who had denied Jesus, who had gone back to fishing, now preaching boldly to the skeptical crowds.

People responding to Peter's message, saying, "Brethren, what shall we do?" and Peter replying, "Repent, and be baptized every one of you in the name of Jesus Christ for the forgiveness of your sins; and you shall receive the gift of the Holy Spirit" (Acts 2:37-38).

Pentecost Is Preparation

Eighth graders meeting together each week after Easter; studying the church that began at Pentecost; studying a church in Ithaca, New York; discovering their part in that church.

These young persons committing themselves to Jesus Christ, the head of the church; and deciding to follow him, symbolizing their decision by baptism.

Group members now choosing personal ways to share their self-discovery and commitment with the congregation: writing a prayer or litany, making a banner, preparing a skit or dramatic reading, rehearsing voices and instruments.

Older youth, baptized the year before, becoming sponsors of the candidates for baptism: supporting, sharing, encouraging.

Youth groups and their leaders planning a church breakfast, coming to the church building on Saturday to hang balloons and streamers in the social hall, sharing the excitement of a celebration-to-come.

Pentecost Is a Breakfast-Celebration

The whole church from babies to older people, gathering together in one place.

Singing, "This is the day that the Lord has made, let us rejoice and be glad in it. . . . This is the day all the world is new, let us rejoice and be glad. . . ."

A banner, shaped like a fish, with pictures of what the church is—baptism, Communion, helping one another, the cross, a body of people of all colors gathered around the Bible—made by the junior choir.

Eating cornflakes topped with ice cream and strawberries—for breakfast!

Sponsors introducing the baptismal candidates, telling of their participation in the church: singing in the choir, helping in the nursery or kitchen or library, helping with "meals on wheels."

Church members welcoming the young people soon to be baptized, sharing memories of their own baptisms, revealing who they were and who they have become, sharing what the church has come to mean to them.

Uniting in a litany:
    The church is quiet sanctuary.
    The church is the noisy street.
    The church is peace.
    The church is conflict.
    The church is prayer.
    The church is protest.
    The church is commitment.
    The church is building.
    The church is for respectable people.

The church is for failures, dropouts, and sinners.
The church is tradition.
The church is revolution.
The church is grace and salvation.
The church is mission and ministry.
The church is a ship.
The church is a basin and a towel.
The church is all of these and more. Different ideas about the nature of the church are a part of its nature. But whether the church is quiet, peace, prayer, and refuge, or conflict, commitment, searing fire, and mission, the church must always be servant.
The world is hungry, hurting, killing, dying, confused, confusing, sorrowing, suffering—but it's the only world we've got—
And we are the only church that's here!

Joining hands and singing, "We are one in the Spirit, we are one in the Lord."

Pentecost Is Worship in the Sanctuary

Two red banners framing the opened baptistry window, one showing the symbol of the dove, the other the symbol of flames.

The words of God's promise, spoken through his prophet, Joel:
"And it shall come to pass afterward,
 that I will pour out my spirit on all flesh;
 your sons and your daughters shall prophesy,
 your old men shall dream dreams,
 and your young men shall see visions."
(Joel 2:28)

Those who are about to be baptized reading the story of Pentecost, leading a responsive reading, sharing a litany of thanksgiving.

Singing, "There's a church within us, O Lord"; singing of potential, of fire for new life, of building the church with our lives, of finding ourselves united as Christ's church in the world.

Candidates for baptism, now in white robes, approaching the baptistry.

The ordinance of baptism:
Question to the candidate:
Do you believe in Jesus Christ, the Son of God, and confess him to be your friend and Savior?
Question to the congregation:
Do you accept _____'s affirmation of faith and promise to help and support his (her) intentions to live this affirmation to the best of his (her) ability?
Congregation's response:
We do. _____, you are the salt of the earth. Always flavor it with Jesus' love. You are the light of the world. Let your light shine before others that they will see the good you do and praise God.

New persons in Christ coming up out of the water, the pastor tenderly drying their faces.

The choir singing a verse from a hymn after each baptism.

Members of the congregation coming up after the service to embrace the newly baptized young people.

Rediscovering that God never leaves his church without the gift of the Holy Spirit, which is joy and newness, peace and unity, love and service.

Model for Staffing Programs

INTERGENERATIONAL TEACHING TEAMS—THEY REALLY WORK [24]
by Richard Rusbuldt

"I learned more in this year of teaching than in all my other years in the Sunday church school." So stated a teen member of an Intergenerational Teaching Team (ITT) as she reached the end of her one-year contract. Two years of ITT pilots in Southeast Pennsylvania have convinced us that there are many educational advantages to ITTs; there can also be several problems.

Intergenerational Teaching Teams are church school teaching teams composed of at least one teenager and adult. The goal of this

[24] Reprinted from *Baptist Leader*, July, 1976, pp. 57-59.

program is for each ITT to be an effective teaching team that provides equal roles for teens and adults. There are many other types of youth/adult teaching teams, but invariably the role of the teen in them is that of a "second-class" teacher, or, as I often call them, "flunkies." They do such things as empty the wastebaskets, capture the children in the hall, clean up paint and other spilled things, and take the pupils to the bathroom. What makes ITTs different are the *equal* roles of the youth and adult team members.

If teens in your church are eager to assume a responsible role in Christian education and if adults are willing to welcome them as equal partners in teaching, then an ITT will meet your needs. I have observed ITTs composed of one teen and one adult, one adult and two teens, two adults and two teens, and two adults and three teens. All were very effective in carrying out their respective teaching responsibilities. Teen members can be junior high or senior high youth, depending on the interest level and maturity of the teen and the needs of the classes being considered for an ITT.

The most important element of ITTs is the people who compose the team. So, before you even begin to think about the possibilities of an ITT for your church, consider these two points of caution:

1. Not every adult teacher is ready for or capable of a meaningful ITT experience.
2. Not every teenager is ready for, wants, or should have an ITT experience.

If you do have the adults and youth who are ready, then where do you begin? After a board or committee of Christian education decides to begin an ITT program, the first step is to select an ITT manager. This person could be the leader development chairperson on your board or committee or perhaps a capable leader co-opted from your fellowship. We learned from our testing that someone *must* be involved on a regular basis to manage the program, including recruiting, enabling, advising, and evaluating. Only in this way can the ITTs work effectively.

Recruitment for ITTs begins by determining which adult teachers or adult teaching teams are willing and ready for an ITT experience. Superintendents, departmental superintendents, and board of Christian education members should participate in this analysis with the ITT manager. The process of selecting and recruiting teens should allow for input from youth advisers, youth teachers, the pastor, and the board of Christian education member with youth responsibilities. When beginning the ITT program, it is best to select both the teens and the adults. When the program is better known and understood by your teachers and congregation, perhaps you can then ask for volunteers.

When you are ready to form ITTs, two things need to happen. First, a contract needs to be written and signed by the participants. We discovered that written contracts which clearly spelled out expectations were most effective. The contracts usually last a year, although this can be flexible. As each ITT is formed, its members agree to work together for six weeks, at which time they will evaluate their ITT and decide if it should continue. It is better to change the teams that are not working out at this point than to struggle along with an ineffective ITT which may hurt both teens and adults, to say nothing of the pupils!

Second, there needs to be some preparation. Possibly several nearby churches can cluster to begin the ITT program. An evening (or two) of team building is a must for all ITT teams. A skilled leader can assist the ITTs in experiencing some team building. Expectations need to be discussed openly, trust levels enhanced, and confidence instilled in the ITTs in these sessions. This step is a *must!*

As you might have guessed, the biggest problem faced by ITTs was that of planning and evaluating together. In a couple of cases, adults not wholly committed to the "equal teen/adult role" tended to "do their own thing" in terms of preparation and bring the teen on board later. However, when the adult teacher(s) was fully committed to the ITT concept and goal, and the teens were equally concerned that they be fully involved, time for joint planning and evaluation was found.

One ITT came together for Sunday dinner at the adult team member's home every other week. The meal provided a relaxed setting, and good planning and evaluation took place; this was a solid team! Others met at various times—for a while at the close of the morning experiences, after school, in the evenings, on Sunday afternoon, etc. One team could not get together in a "face-to-face" session, so the telephone opened the door to planning and evaluating on a regular basis. Several hours were spent each week on the phone; they were an extremely effective team, too!

After six weeks of ITT, one teacher described the teen's role: "Our teen member is a full-fledged teacher. She gives input to our sessions, takes charge of storytime, leads singing, helps in activities, and is on a one-to-one basis with behavior problems that need special assistance."

After a year of ITT, another teacher said: "Most teens would much rather participate in a leader role than be passive onlookers. Our teen teacher has worked with individual children, has given other leaders input, and has helped the children relax by involving them in some energetic games and exercises which I can't do."

A teen said: "I learn from teaching. I really have a place on Sunday morning instead of just being another member in a class. I know that I am getting more out of the Sunday school hour by teaching."

Still another teen: "This experience is satisfactory because I don't have to go into the senior high class. I don't like lectures and prefer the active participating that teaching gives. I feel I'm doing something."

Problems? Weaknesses? Yes, there are some. We have already mentioned that getting together to plan and evaluate is one of the most difficult problems to overcome. Others include the following:

1. Youth are deprived of a peer group experience on Sunday morning.

2. Youth can be exploited to "fill the gaps" on Sunday morning.

3. You can get the "wrong" teen with the "wrong" adult and vice versa.

4. Youth are quickly discouraged if it is not a true *team* experience. Dominating adults don't "make it" with teens!

5. Placing more than one teen on a team can be a problem if they are not compatible or perhaps are too much so (boyfriend—girlfriend, etc.).

6. Pupils' needs must come first, not the needs of the teens or the ITT concept itself.

7. The needs of children especially call for understanding, planning, preparation, and patience; teens often lack experience and maturity and find it difficult to set aside time for planning.

Although we have talked only of ITTs composed of teens and adults—and have only tested on that level—it is important to point out that some effective teaching with adult classes could take place by creating teaching teams with different ages of adults on them. There are some serious communication gaps in our churches between the young adults and the middle-aged and between the middle-aged adults and the older adults. Providing mixed teaching teams on these levels provides for the cross-fertilization of ideas, relationships, and feelings which are all valuable for your church. I also recommend ITTs (with teens) to teach adult classes.

Written evaluations about the ITT program have been very positive. Most of the teens involved think it is one of the best things that has happened to them in their growing-up experience in the church. Having observed many strengths and a few weaknesses, we feel certain that Intergenerational Teaching Teams can provide a fresh and vital approach to creating new life and vitality in our traditional church schools.

Basic Assumptions Which Underlie the ITT Program

1. Teens have something to give, i.e., talents, a faith, vigor, creativity, freshness, questions!
2. After being in the role of learner for years, *many* youth are *bored*. (If you doubt this, test the assumption on your junior and senior highs.)
3. Youth are a part of an action generation; some *want* to get involved.
4. A change of pace from learner to teacher role may change the attitudes and perspectives of teens, thus establishing new meaning for them in the church.
5. More learning takes place through the teacher role than the pupil role.
6. Youth need to assume responsibility.
7. Several communication gaps can be bridged, including: children-teens; teens-adults; adults-children; adults-adults.
8. Teens need to test their faith in a realistic setting; the teaching role often provides the reality context.
9. Many teens want to grow and develop in their relationship to their church, their faith, and others.
10. Each church needs to work at the long-range development of their leaders. This is an investment in the future.
11. Working as teaching teams is more effective than working as individual teachers.
12. The age mix of teachers provides more creativity, different levels of communication, and a freshness not always found in other types of teaching patterns.
13. The church should prepare its young to teach, not push them into teaching roles later on.

List of Alternate Models

So You Want to Try Learning Centers	38
"We Decided to Try Learning Centers"	42
Church School Doesn't Want to Die!	48
Church Schools Don't Need to Die	51
Institute for Creative Living	57
Retreats • An Answer to Your Youth Group Slump?	58
A Christian Nursery Center	62
The Learning Community	66
Vacation Church School Goes Under . . . Water	70
Local Church Camping	74
Study Tours	75
Tripping with Young People	76
An Intergenerational Sunday Church School	78
A Family Cluster Experience	82
Adolescents Look at Family Clusters	85
The Gathering Place	90
A Saturday Church School	93
"Big Tuesday"	93
A Creative Approach to Scheduling in the Church	96
Festival of Faith	98
Celebrating Pentecost	101
Intergenerational Teaching Teams—They Really Work	105

Bibliography

Interpretation

Blazier, Kenneth D., *Building an Effective Church School:* Guide for the Superintendent & Board of Christian Education. Valley Forge: Judson Press, 1976. $1.95

Cully, Iris V., *New Life for Your Sunday School.* New York: Hawthorn Books, Inc., 1976. $5.95

Duckert, Mary, *Open Education Goes to Church.* Philadelphia: The Westminster Press, 1976. $3.45

Learning Centers

Ishler, Richard E.; Ishler, Margaret F.; and Lamb, Phyllis, *First Steps to Open Classrooms in the Church.* Chicago: The Arizona Experiment (National Teacher Education Project), 1974. $1.95. Order from publisher, 35 E. Wacker Dr., Chicago, IL 60601.

The Joy of Learning, Using Learning Centers. 75 frame color filmstrip with record and two scripts. $5.95. Order from Presbyterian Church, U.S., Material Distribution Service, 341 Ponce de Leon Ave., NE, Atlanta, GA 30308.

The Learning Center Approach in Church Education (a pamphlet). $1.25. Order from DECEE, Box 179, St. Louis, MO 63166.

Learning Centers: Here's How! (a packet, price to be determined). Available through Literature Service, Judson Book Stores: Valley Forge, PA 19481; 670 E. Butterfield Rd., Lombard, IL 60148; 816 S. Figueroa St., Los Angeles, CA 90017.

Sprague, Ruth; and Goddard, Carolyn, *Learning Center Approach Revisited* (a pamphlet). $1.50. Order from DECEE, Box 179, St. Louis, MO 63166.

Using Learning Centers in Church Education. Design No. 1 (a pamphlet). $1.55. Order from Judson Book Stores. Valley Forge, PA 19481; 670 E. Butterfield Rd., Lombard, IL 60148; 816 S. Figueroa St., Los Angeles, CA 90017.

Retreats and Other Models

An Inquiry Approach to Teaching (a pamphlet). $1.25. Order from Judson Book Stores: Valley Forge, PA 19481; 670 E. Butterfield Rd., Lombard, IL 60148; 816 S. Figueroa St., Los Angeles, CA 90017.

Nelson, Virgil; and Nelson, Lynn, *Retreat Handbook*. Valley Forge; Judson Press, 1976. $5.95

Planning Intergenerational Experiences, LS15-323. $3.95. Order from Judson Book Stores: Valley Forge, PA 19481; 670 E. Butterfield Rd., Lombard, IL 60148; 816 S. Figueroa St., Los Angeles, CA 90017.

Teacher Preparation

Goldman, Ronald, *Readiness for Religion*. New York: The Seabury Press, Inc., 1970. $3.95

Holcomb, Jerry, *Team Teaching with the Scotts and Bartons*. Valley Forge: Judson Press, 1968. $2.50

MacInnes, Donald I., *Team Teaching*. Audio Cassette, leader's guide, and overhead project transparencies. $10.95. Order from National Teacher Education Project, 35 E. Wacker Dr., Chicago, IL 60601.